OVERCOMING THE
ARCHON
THROUGH
ALCHEMY

JOHN KREITER

Overcoming the Archon Through Alchemy

Copyright © 2017 John Kreiter

www.johnkreiter.com

All rights reserved. No part of this book shall be reproduced, stored in a retrieval system, or transmitted by any means—electronic, mechanical, photocopying, recording, or otherwise—without written permission from the publisher, except for the inclusion of brief quotations in a review.

Authors and the publisher shall have neither liability nor responsibility to any person or entity with respect to any loss or damages arising from the information contained in this book.

Table of Contents

Introduction 1

CHAPTER 1 Beginning at the Beginning 13

CHAPTER 2 The Alchemist's View 35

CHAPTER 3 The Holy Trinity 55

CHAPTER 4 The Power of the IN Polarity 77

   Exercise: Energy Absorption Technique 94

   Exercise: Discovering and Using Your Psychic Energy Pumps 98

CHAPTER 5 Into the VOID 101

   Exercise 1: First Level of Energetic Containment 117

   Exercise 2: Second Level of Energetic Containment 125

CHAPTER 6 Going OUT 135

   Focused Attention 149

      Exercise: Visualization Through Focused Attention 152

   Breathing OUT 162

   Emotion 164

CHAPTER 7 The Supreme Ultimate and Refining the IN Polarity 167

   Exercise: Negative Energy Absorption 181

CHAPTER 8, PART 1 Yang 193

CHAPTER 8, PART 2 Desire Without Compromise
.... 209

CHAPTER 8, PART 3 Dare to Desire 223

CHAPTER 9 VOID the Final Frontier 241

   Exercise: Energy Containment While In a Large Crowd (Energetic Containment Level 1) 248

   Exercise: Silencing the Mind through Melatonin Build-up (Energetic Containment Level 2) 255

Conclusion 263

Glossary 271

> **Thou must part him in three**
> **And then knit him as the Trinity**
> **And make them all but one**
> **Lo here is the Philosophers Stone**
> *RIPLEY SCROLL,*
> *BY THE CHANON OF BRIDLINGTON*

Introduction

Better to fight for something than live for nothing.
GEORGE S. PATTON

What counts is not necessarily the size of the dog in the fight - it's the size of the fight in the dog.
DWIGHT D. EISENHOWER

If we look around this world, especially now that we have so much access to information, things can seem very chaotic and downright crazy at times. Whatever you might think about the state of the world right now, one can make the case that everything changes, and that those changes seem to be happening at a faster and faster pace.

I will argue in this book that these changes are the result of an energetic flux, that has both internal (subjective) and external (from the world at large) origins. I will try to show as clearly as possible that a great deal of this flux is quite negative to humanity, and that the origins of this negative aspect of the flux of life, is the result of a titanic force that does not have humanity's best interest in mind.

But I will also show the reader that humanity is not helpless against this titanic force, that through the correct use of certain energetic techniques, this dark force can actually be used in a transformative way to get all the things that you may desire and to break free from the oppressive aspects of this life that we all share.

This book then, is about fighting back and beating a global system that traps the average person in a cage without walls, and in a life with little personal fulfillment.

There have been many books written about how to use your mind to change your life and your reality. Many of these books will tell you that your entire life is the result of internal subjective states; the beliefs, thoughts, and ideas that occupy your mind.

There are a number of books that are very helpful and give people hope, and in the best of times they introduce techniques that people can use to better their lives. Often times though, these books can be a bit disappointing because the changes that people want don't come very quickly or they don't come at all.

People are left wondering why certain techniques work sometimes to some degree.

They sometimes wonder why it is impossible to fight against the system. Even when they are given strategies on how to stop paying attention to the system, so that they may break free from it, they wonder why these techniques fail. They wonder why it is impossible to escape this oppressive cage without walls, and why it is impossible to escape those people that make up the core of this seemingly broken system.

They also wonder why their attention fails. They wonder why it is so difficult to maintain their thoughts focused on one subject over time; even when those thoughts are about things that they really like or love.

Such questions can have people wondering if they are doing something wrong or if the techniques that they are being taught are not quite right. Many contemplate the possibility that they are being told only some of the truth, and as a result often waste a great deal of time looking for that perfect technique that will be able to get them what they want through the power of their Will and the focus of their attention.

This book will provide the answers to all these questions, AND it will also provide a functional way to change your life for the better through the power of thoughts, energetic re-direction, and focused attention.

In this book, I show you how to do this by introducing a very ancient system of energetic manipulation referred to as Alchemy. And unlike most of the literature that you can find on Alchemy, there are no hidden codes in this book that will only allow the initiated to learn the real truth. This book is not made up of half-truths, metaphors, or riddles. It plainly explains how to use Alchemical energetic techniques.

In that sense, it could be said that this book is about uncovering the truth, and using the knowledge gained to beat a system that is designed to take more from you than you could ever get back from it.

This book tells the truth without compromise and it is important that I begin to relate some of this truth right here in this introduction. In this way, if you wish to read further then you will understand plainly what this book is about, and if you want to put the book down and move on, then you can do so freely.

The first truth that I must relate is that we are all surrounded by infinity. As you look around, you might think that you are a being that lives in a world surrounded by objects and that you are an object yourself, albeit a sentient one.

Alchemists though, discovered a very long time ago that we are all lost in a perceptive illusion. This illusion hides the fact that there are no objects Out There, there is only energy. While some could argue that there are certain energetic conglomerations that might act upon humanity in a way that we have learned to describe as objects, the fundamental reality is that those objects (and the solidity that we ascribe to them) is an illusion...an imposed illusion!

Alchemists would say that we are in fact surrounded by infinity, which could more succinctly be described as an immeasurable Dark Sea.

The second Alchemical finding that I must relate is that we **humans are not the apex predators that we think we are**. Our conceptions of reality tell us that we are a sentient object surrounded by other objects that are not sentient like we are, and that within this realm of lesser objects we are the most powerful creatures because of this supposed greater awareness that we enjoy; the top predatory creature that preys on the rest of the world.

The Alchemical perspective though, is that we are not this top predator by a long shot, and that there are many creatures Out There that now consider us food. These predatory creatures that consume man, the supposed apex predator, are for the most part completely outside of the human perceptual radar. This is so because these life forms are not considered possible in a world view that only believes in the power of objects.

You see, these predatory creatures are non-organic, that is: they are not objects as we understand the term, and are therefore beyond current rational perception. These beings could be said to be life forms that are not bound by biology, and are in essence a type of energetic conglomeration that does not require a vibratory frequency range we refer to as physical form.

These creatures vary greatly in shape and size and there is indeed an incredible variety of them just on this Earth. These creatures can vary in size from something as small as a goldfish, to beings as large as the clouds in the sky. These beings of course are not completely outside of the human perceptive world, and indeed there are a number of occult groups and occult practices that are specifically geared towards the interaction with these beings in order to gain power and knowledge.

In this book, we will be discussing and looking into one particular non-organic energetic conglomeration. This conglomeration could be said to be the biggest non-organic life form within our human sphere. This non-organic life form has been known by many names throughout history, but the one that perhaps captures the true reality of this titanic force the best is the name: Archon.

You might wonder what all this has to do with fighting back against the system, getting those things you desire through mind power, and Alchemy in particular?

The answer to this can be found by uncovering the greatest secret in alchemy, which is this:

Alchemy is solely based on techniques designed to overcome the Archonic predatory non-organic life force that is now consuming the energetic essence of all humankind. Alchemy therefore concerns itself completely with the accumulation of the energetic essence of the individual human being.

Once an Alchemist has acquired enough of this energy, which is being taken from humanity without their consent, Alchemy concerns itself with how to redeploy these gains in order to

change every aspect of the Alchemist's life; both on a material and spiritual level.

If all this seems a little overwhelming right now, please note that I describe all of this in much more detail in the book. Beyond this, I present VERY powerful Alchemical techniques that should allow you to finally put it all together, as it were. This explanation, plus the accompanying techniques provide the FULL answer to what I have discussed thus far:

- The truth about the great Archon and the reason for all the strife and pain in this world
- The truth about the energetic essence of humanity: How this energy is absorbed and created, and how this energy moves within and without the human energetic structure

and it will also provide ways to:

- Use the power of the mind to change your personal objective reality
- Use 'Will Force' to redirect the people around you so that they either help you, or don't interfere with the life you want to live
- Gain more power, and wisdom, so that you may use that power wisely
- Become wealthy both materially and spiritually

- Stop the flux of life and attain what some Eastern schools refer to as Samadhi and eventual Nirvana if you so desire
- Move beyond this world into other dimensional states

One could say that this book begins by explaining the power of causality; first from the regular human perspective, the perspective of the object filled universe which could be referred to as the mechanical view.

But then then it continues by introducing a new type of causality which in many ways is profoundly different from the one that humanity is using at this moment in time. This new type of causality is the Alchemical perspective, one which is completely reliant on energetic movements. From this new Alchemical cause-and-effect perspective, which is based completely on an energetic view of reality, we see the world in a whole 'new light'.

This new light allows us to begin to discuss and apply a new way of doing things. This energetic view provides answers that explain why things are the way they are right now; it explains what is really going on in the world. And furthermore, it makes available a better methodology for acting in this world.

And indeed, this book does provide a way to fight against those forces that are now engaged in the act of enslaving humanity, forces that have been active in this world for millennia and seem to be close to consolidating their power on this Earth forever.

Most importantly, this book will reveal the Grand and Holy Trinity of Alchemy! It reveals how to use its secrets to extract, purify and transmute energy in order to break the chains of enslavement. The secrets of the Holy Trinity of Alchemy allow a human being to develop true control over all aspects of his or her life, and allow that person to fight against the oppression of the human zombies, that now rule this world in the name of the Great Archon.

As the world continues its game of dystopian monopoly, I will show you how to walk off the board and poke at it until you get what you want. Indeed, I am not only going to show you the edges of the board and how to step off it, I am going to show you how to move the monopoly pieces with the power of your Intent alone.

That's what alchemists do. They show that, when we strive to become better than we are, everything around us becomes better, too.
PAULO COELHO, THE ALCHEMIST

CHAPTER 1
Beginning at the Beginning

In order to begin to understand the Alchemical perspective which follows, and how to use its secrets in order to begin to control our energetic and objective fate, it is best that we begin at the beginning as they say. Such a beginning means that we should start by examining the modern world from the normal human Cognitive Stance.

Referred to as the mundane world view by some, this world view is the rational one, the one that the majority of human beings on this planet share. The average skeptical person believes this to be the only real view, the only logical one, the only one that really counts, since any other world view is to them utter delusion.

This normal, rational, world view tells us that we are part of a very intricate society made of things. The average rational world view, believes that man is an object surrounded by other objects. Rationality, which represents sanity and correct thinking in our modern times, is developed and organized through the use of a type of narrow logic that is based solely on a mechanical interpretation of reality.

This mechanistic interpretation of reality posits that we are meat machines, surrounded by hard non-sentient objects, and that it is only through reason that we can function effectively in the world. Man is seen as the apex creature, the only truly sentient being on this planet.

This limited Cognitive Structure imposes a limited logical framework on the average person, and this framework rules the many diverse sciences and philosophies that we now practice. Even though certain branches of science, using more sophisticated logic, have been discovering and revealing some of the great mystery of the world and the great folly of the average Cognitive Stance, humanity continues to act like a schizophrenic madman.

Physics reveals a world of energy and seemingly magical interconnectedness, biology discovers fact upon fact that shows the inadequacy of modern evolutionary causality models, chemistry begins to run straight into insurmountable walls as it tries unsuccessfully to figure out certain atomic interactions, but humanity deeply stuck in a rational stance, closes its eyes, shuts the door and puts its weight against it; like a novice wizard that accidentally opened up a hidden door that looks out into infinity and madness.

This rational perspective is not all bad; such a rational stance has benefits. It allows us all to share a reality in which we can work together towards a relatively common goal, but such a Cognitive Position means that the average person sees life as being cold, predictable, and full of limits.

And so, like a schizophrenic fool, going from moments of brilliance to moments of true idiocy, humanity plows forth, encumbered by its latest religion: rationality. And it is from this Cognitive Position which is referred to as sanity and COMMON sense, that we look upon this world.

Even though this chapter deals with understanding the modern world from the Rational world view, it is important that we define the term 'Cognitive Position', because this shapeless and currently unmeasurable reality construction point plays such an important role in all human affairs.

We can define Cognitive Position this way:

The organizational blueprint that defines how an aware being structures thoughts, experience and sensual data. This position is the result of humanity's biological makeup, beliefs, energetic level, **AND external influences**. There are an infinite number of cognitive positions, and each one provides a different world view that can be somewhat different or completely different from any other. Changing Cognitive Positions can allow a person to see/experience and act upon the world in different ways.

A small shift in Cognitive Positions can be achieved through a change in beliefs, because beliefs are the underlying foundations that cause us to think, act, and perceive in a certain way. Each belief gestalt brings with it, its own logical structure which basically means that each belief system creates its own causality matrix; its own idea of what cause and effect entail.

Rationalists will tell you that there is only one kind of logic: theirs. Everything else being delusion and insanity. But the reality is that there are many types of logic, something that we will explore further in Chapter 2.

An example of such a small shift in belief and therefore causality model, can be observed by contemplating the different Cognitive Positions of rationalistic atheism and religious fervor. These are two separate Cognitive Positions that provide a completely different world view, slightly different logical (that is, causality) structures, and therefore completely different ways to act upon the world.

While this is a small difference in Cognitive Position (in that both share nearly identical sensual data patterns from a human biological perspective) such sensual data can be structured in completely different ways. This means that certain thoughts and sense data will be ignored while other thoughts and sense data will be focused upon completely. A belief structure then, is like a large sieve that only allows certain data to go through while completely blocking all the others.

If as we continue this example, we can imagine what these two individuals might see when they both look at the same boulder out in the middle of a barren field.

The rationalistic atheist might see:

- granite or granitoid
- one object (a rock) on top of another object (the Earth)
- The end result of cold and highly efficient geological process that affects all objects

within space and gives the impression of sentient order.

A fervent religionist might see:

- a miracle
- the will of God
- A big rock created by God in the beginning of time. Interconnection brought together through the great power of spirit as it provides hope, direction and a future for those that follow the unshakable law of being.

Same place, same boulder, different mental structures.

A very large variance in Cognitive Positions on the other hand, can reveal wholly different worlds; no more boulder, totally different place!

From an Alchemical perspective then, Cognitive Positions create reality, not the other way around.

And from the Cognitive Position that now rules most of the Western world (rationality), we can interpret what this modern world has become:

As the human population grows and as technology advances at an increasing rate, we find ourselves in a world where you can't even cough without somebody catching it on video and sharing it with the rest of humanity. With a single click, we are connected to billions of other minds, and those minds are not always interested in friendly interaction; they are actually most often interested in 'pushing' their agendas and opinions on others.

'Political Correctness' is the newest religious buzz phrase in this modern rational world, and using its dictums, people are forced to follow a certain life strategy. If they deviate from this correct way of being, a person can be punished by their peers or by the state. Thanks to the interconnectedness that modern technology allows, this highly systematized 'push' to have everyone become a loving all-inclusive herd, has begun the conversion of billions, and has become one of the biggest memes on this planet.

Many say that in this time in history people have the greatest individual freedoms, and for the most part can express their opinions and ideas freely in the world...certainly it seems easy enough to get an online media account and start ranting.

And yet in no time in history have so many embraced and been influenced by belief structures, that would have them give up their individuality and share one mind and one social ideal.

Belief structures (or memes), thanks to the interconnected super highway that is the internet, now have a power that would have seemed impossible just a few decades ago. And while the benefits of this interconnection must not be overlooked, it is also worth noting that this web of connections now sways human opinion, through the direct control of what humans experience and therefore believe; in ways that are quite literally beyond Orwellian sophistication.

From a rational perspective, this incredible growth and change in humanity is the result of natural evolution. It is generally accepted that it is evolution and the process of natural selection that is responsible for what we human beings are now, and what we may become in the future. Evolutionary theory is a most logical premise and you will find that Alchemy does not dismiss this 'transmutative' model completely. It is actually the case that the science of Alchemy agrees with the basics of this process of evolution, which it refers to as transmutation, and only finds fault in the very limited causality models used by the modern scientific establishment to try and understand this process.

Evolutionary theory tells us that things evolve through a gradual process. From a purely rational (that is modern) scientific perspective, evolution is seen as gradual mechanism that affects populations, not individuals. An evolutionary change therefore is a 'heritable' change that is transmitted from one generation to the next through a medium identified as genetic material.

One could define this process more simply by saying that it is the copying or transference of certain genetic material with the addition of variation and selection.

Such a process can be used to explain, with some tweaking and the overlooking of a great deal of data, how the whole of this world evolved from one thing to another, and how it is that we have arrived at this spot in time with man supposedly as the apex creature on this planet.

It is quite simply a cause and effect model that uses a type of mechanistic logic to explain our place in the universe. The rational mind accepts all its premises and with it we could, if we had the time, explain how it is that humanity is in this state, and what the future might hold for all of us.

Unfortunately, this gene based evolutionary process can give us some perspective, but aside from telling us why humans 'can' engage in such complex mental actions, it can't really explain Political Correctness, or why we seem to be at the nexus of great societal change.

For such an understanding, we need to consult a more recent brother of genetic (or biological) evolution called Memetics.

Most people tend to think of memes as fads, which I suppose is a relatively accurate definition, however this definition does not even hint at the incredible power that the meme has in all human affairs. Indeed, a meme can be defined simply as that which is imitated from person to person; which on the surface does not seem like a very big deal.

But if we look back at the definition of evolution, we find an amazing correlation between genes and memes.

Since biological evolutionary theory is quite simply the copying of genetic material from one generation to the next, while variation and selection are present, one could say that the meme is a different type of copying process that serves the same purpose as genetic material!

The truly incredible part is that this new copying mechanism that produces design through variation and selection just like genes, is completely information based; there is absolutely nothing physical about it, it is a completely subjective event that later produces objective results in the host, without the need for genetic transference at all.

Using Memetics we can, through a rational scientific model, examine the modern world and the future of humanity. We can see how memes, which are belief structures that are being passed from one person to another almost like a biological contagion, have shaped all of our known history. A religion or a political ideology for example can be considered memes, very large and complex memes, but memes none the less.

And it can be seen that such large and powerful memes, like a religion or a political ideology, seem to exist like living organisms that have the need to propagate themselves, going from one human mind to the next.

A meme then can dedicate some or all of the resources of the host body, to try and replicate itself in more and more minds. The meme grows in size and power as it affects more and more human minds, and then goes about using this added power to grow further, get stronger, and live longer.

Sounds almost like a zombie apocalypse, or perhaps the plot line to some kind of sci-fi 'pod people' movie, doesn't it? And yet it is a good cause and effect model that is being studied quite seriously by scientists all over the world.

I wonder if you caught the one very scary phrase from above? The one phrase that should scare you, it certainly scares me quite a lot, is:

'dedicates some or all of the resources of the host body to try and replicate itself'.

That's right; a meme doesn't weave its way into your brain and then sits there peacefully and quietly as you make your way through life. A meme, just like a biological invader, actually uses the host body to try and replicate itself. It quite literally forces the body to go out and infect as many people as it can. So just like a particular genetic trait, it can be said that a meme is only as successful as its host's ability to replicate it.

Think about the 'Political Correctness' meme for example. When it invades a certain brain, when someone converts to that particular belief structure, that person usually begins to engage in a quite deliberate propaganda campaign in order to convert and enforce all the dictums that this new belief structure demands. If this person is famous or powerful in some way, then this new belief structure will most likely acquire many new converts as this person uses his or her vast resources to convert others. If, on the other hand, the infected host is of a reserved nature and does not have a great deal of social power, then this meme will most likely not have as much success at spreading itself further. The meme then is only as successful as the host(s) that it manages to infect.

But whatever the case, the true power of this meme comes from its ability to use the host's resources to its own ends.

Just like a biological infection, some might be infected by the Politically Correct meme and might not suffer greatly from this infection at all. While there might be others that might become truly sick and lose a great deal of life force and perhaps even their lives as they try desperately to convert/infect others. Indeed, a meme seems to share many similarities with a virus, and interestingly viruses are now being used as a way to introduce new genetic material into host bodies.

The meme then can be said to be one of the most powerful evolutionary forces shaping the human race. It infects host bodies just like a virus, introducing new material that then can cause severe mutations in the host mind. These mental mutations divert some or all of the resources available to the host and force that host mind to do what it can to 'push' that meme into the minds of others.

Memetics then is an amazing science that can help us to understand what is going on in the world right now. Unfortunately, it suffers from one rather large problem:

Scientist can't measure the true complexity of human thought and the subjective realm in which these thoughts exist.

Since Memetics deals with something that cannot truly be measured, it is not taken very seriously. This is so because the rational Cognitive Stance demands such objective measurements; **all that can't be measured, that can't be defined as an object, is not real.**

This means that while in this chapter I strive to provide a rational explanation for the world as it is today and as it might be in the future, such conceptions might not be truly possible because of the highly limited rational perspective. Memetics gives us a clue, but it is flawed from a rational perspective because of its limited ability to measure what it studies. Also, while Memetics might be able to tell us how memes can shape the world, it can't tell us where these memes come from, why some become more powerful than others and why some fade away while others thrive (for such explanations we will need to wait until the next chapter where the Alchemical Cognitive Stance is discussed).

You might quite rationally believe perhaps that there is one simple antidote to harmful memes like Political Correctness. One would imagine that you could just unplug yourself from all this social media mess and that would be the end of it. Unfortunately, such a task is most often a near impossibility, since more and more of us now need this technological interconnection in order to do our jobs and get along in life.

Perhaps we can all do with a lot less social media, and if we try we can certainly reduce our intake of opinion upon opinion, mixed with healthy doses of repetition and outright lies, that are now part and parcel of even supposedly unbiased news organizations.

But even those that can completely detach themselves from the drone of the hive mind, cannot completely run away from the world altogether, because that world is full of an ever-growing population that is itself infected by the many memes of the times. These memes, which are in essence whole belief structures that are passed on from one person to another in a viral like way, change those ever-growing populations and quite literally turn those infected into robots/zombies that serve this powerful new belief structure.

These robots serve this new meme in the only way that such a meme could be served; they provide these new memes with energy.

As discussed above, some adherents of this new meme, that is robots/zombies, give up some of their energy, while others give up almost all of their life force in the cause of this new, seemingly all-powerful belief. Most people are aware of the fact that they are giving up energy to this new meme, which they often call a cause or an undeniable fact, and most people are ok with that because they think it is the 'correct' thing to do. What they fail to understand is that human thought and attention are very powerful commodities that are being used to feed structures that do not have humanity's best interest in any way.

Certainly, many who have become complete adherents of a new meme, would give up their life and souls in order to 'save the world' and propagate the beliefs and opinions that these memes advocate. Convincing such people that they have truly given up their lives for new beliefs that are usually not interested in their individual well-being, is unfortunately irrelevant, because most people are not interested in hearing your opinion, only in propagating theirs. And to be fair, our beliefs are no better than theirs, no matter what our own personal memes might push us to say or do!

The great desire to try and change another person's belief structure is just a symptom of viral infection, caused by whatever meme we might be infected with ourselves.

Changing someone's mind, is like trying to tell a complete rationalist that if he were only to not believe in gravity, he could walk on clouds. At best, you would be ignored or told to get lost, at worst you would be insulted and punched in the face. Just imagine what the social media war (I mean debate) between those who believe in gravity and those that don't might be like. Imagine the marches, the knuckle fights, the riots, the online rallies, the groups and organizations created, the campaigns promoting the wearing of certain colors or logos. The corporate and governmental cabals (I mean organizations) promoting one side of the belief or the other in order to gain greater wealth and power.

And then imagine a most unusual person, a person who has managed to unplug him or herself from this gigantic battle of opposing memes. Can this person be free from the fray? Is this person safe, both energetically and physically?

"No," is the short answer, he or she won't be able to escape for long. As the battle rages and grows, this person will begin to feel the effects both physically and mentally. As more people channel their energy into one belief or the other, the belief structure grows in power and develops a type of self-sustaining drive that becomes stronger and stronger. The force of this belief structure is usually not felt by the average person at first, at least in a conscious way, but a sensitive will feel the thoughts and intent of all those people, and depending on how sensitive this person is, he or she may be assaulted by anxiety, bad dreams, and even feel his or her emotions swaying from one extreme to the other, as little debates rage in his or her head for no real apparent reason.

Such a mass projection of attention by so many people into one particular belief structure will begin to manifest aspects of that structure in the physical world. Such a structure will create new governments, wars, buildings, technology, and scripture. It will change economies and the wealth of nations if it becomes big enough.

Our lone person, the only unplugged human on the planet, will not be able to stay out of this battle any longer, whether he or she is a sensitive or not. Signs of this new belief structure, this meme made concrete, will be everywhere. Jobs, to which this person might need to go to, will change to suit a new standard, and the very cost of food and water might change as a result of this 'new reality'. The people around this lone person will also change, both mentally and physically, and he or she will be forced to convert, act like a convert, or flee.

Looking at this modern world we can see that the great movement of people happening now, as a minor few flee the great concentrations of humanity, and the majority of others flood the 'developed' world. The mass migration of people from the third world into the first is to be expected, indeed it is seen as an inevitable conclusion of great population growth and the scarcity of money and resources.

But is this 'rational' consequence something that has to happen?

As most of those caught in the rationalistic meme would declare; it's just evolution and the laws of supply and demand at work. But does so much misery have to happen for evolution to carry on in its merry way?

This is something that we will look into more deeply in the second chapter. For now let us just realize that modern memes create change that is touted as being 'inevitable' by those very memetic forces (rationality being one of the biggest right now) that are causing all the change in the first place.

While the attribution of everything to memetic forces would be a gross overestimation of human thought power (sorry), I do hope to show you as the book progresses that indeed all of what we see is the result of Internal Action first, which then becomes physical action, objects, and events.

Such an understanding, which I have introduced from a rational perspective using the science of Memetics, can begin the process of great 'illumination', and this process is the first and most precious jewel in the great Alchemical work; it is quite unabashedly the first step in the process of attainment of ILLUMINATUS.

But in order to understand the greater whole of this illumination, we must strive to attain a different Cognitive Position. This is needed because even though the science of Memetics, and certain logical structures that are used in other sciences, can be highly perceptive and most helpful, they fail in one very large respect; they do not reveal the ultimate cause of things.

A rational mind believes that it has all the answers, that it has even the answer for the ultimate cause of things. But from an Alchemical perspective, the rational Cognitive Position is very narrow and the beliefs that drive it block out sensory data that is crucial in understanding what is really going on in this world.

And since knowing the fundamental cause of things is of ultimate importance if we are to continue, I am obliged to present the state of the modern world as it is perceived from a different Cognitive Position.

CHAPTER 2
The Alchemist's View

When an Alchemist sees the world, he or she does not see the same thing that other people do. Actually, it would be more precise to say that for an Alchemist, there are many different ways to view the world, and there is only one that he or she would consider most accurate.

As I have mentioned before, when the average person looks at the world, he or she sees objects. They see concrete obstacles that must be avoided, manipulated, or walked around if necessary. They even see their own bodies (and as an extension they see themselves) as objects that must be worked upon and manipulated in highly mechanical ways. For that reason they have developed all sorts of different mental processes in order to try and deal with the cold mechanical life they perceive.

Alchemists on the other hand, have the possibility of seeing the world in different ways. And of all the ways that are available to them, there is one which is considered the most correct way. This most correct way is: the **Energetic Cognitive Position**.

What this means is that for an Alchemist, life does not have to be about objects at all. Life and reality can be perceived as energy, and when the world is perceived in this way, they realize that it is the fluctuations and alterations of energy that define how we all experience reality. Moreover, since these fluctuations and alterations of energy happen in ways that are not bound by the cause-and-effect models that the modern world accepts as being the only possible ones, Alchemists can experience time in ways that are very difficult for the average person to even conceptualize.

> It is the case that modern human minds have a great fondness for linear sequences. I would argue that because of this there is a great desire within

> even an Alchemist's mind, to try and define the marvels that they are able to perceive within a logical structure, that sometimes borrows from current scientific cause-and-effect models. But such desires, to try and develop a type of sequential logical structure to define the great unknown Out There, are for the most part just indulgences which are not really needed after a certain amount of energetic evolution.
>
> I personally, for example, still NEED (and deeply enjoy) this linear logical framework, and if it wasn't for this personal need, I doubt that I would be able to write these books.

From an energetic perspective, the world is a very strange and infinitely magical place; it certainly does not have the solidity that the average person takes for granted.

An Alchemist sees the world as a churning sea of energy. He or she perceives the world as a Great Dark Sea, a deep and turbulent energetic unknown that both entices the Alchemist, and scares them to their core. From this energetic perspective, human beings are only small bubbles of aware energy, caught within the tides of a Great Dark Unknown.

The energetic perspective, the energetic view, which could be referred to as the fundamental Cognitive Perspective that all Alchemists crave and strive for, does not see objects or people Out There, it only sees fluctuations of vibrating energy. These vibrating fluctuations sometimes separate into different energetic conglomerations that could be said to have shape, but such pooling of energy is just one transitory twist within an infinite tide; and all is part of the Great Dark Sea.

Life, all life in every possible world, from the smallest single cell organisms, to the largest creature imaginable, are all natural bi-products created by the Great Dark Sea as it churns and twist in endless movement. Aware life can be thought of as bubbles of varying size, created across the depth and breadth of the entire sea, just like bubbles might be naturally created within our own seas here on Earth. We human are simply bubbles then, aware life that for a brief moment knows itself as an individual. And like all bubbles, our existence is brief; here one moment and gone the next.

This movement within the tides, as a bubble is created and then is forced to collapse through endless pressure, is what is referred to as an existence or a Life Cycle. But even brief existence is full of hope because each one of these bubbles, or awareness units, has the possibility of evolutionary change and growth.

For the Alchemist, the world is not a hard place where the only change possible is arrived at through physically intensive mechanistic manipulations. Instead everything is fluctuating energy, and the ability to change one thing to another involves different processes, ones that are not so binding or limiting. These processes, do not require tools or mechanics per se, they require the focus and manipulation of energy.

For the Alchemist, 'all' is energy; the only difference is the oscillations of this energy, which can be altered through the manipulation of the Alchemist's awareness. The manipulation of this awareness is made possible through the acquisition and the correct deployment of energy through personal attention.

For an Alchemist, energy is everything; it is how they get things done and it is how they see the world.

From the Alchemist's point of view then, this modern world that seems to be changing at a faster and faster rate is a completely energetic affair. When they see the modern war upon human freedoms and individuality, they do not see memes or belief structures per se; they see fluctuating energy created as a result of:

- the unending movements of the Great Dark Sea
- as a result of human attention and Intent
- and as result of external 'Alien' Intent

From a rational Cognitive Perspective, to contemplate the possibility that there are external forces, and even more incredibly Alien life, that are manipulating humanity in order to consume humanity in the same way that we humans consume cattle, seems totally insane.

But from an Alchemist's point of view, from an energetic point of view, that is exactly what is going on!

The average person might speak of dogmas, of political ideologies, of cause and effect scenarios that are brought about as a result of people waging ideological wars against each other. They may speak of these things because they can see physical wars and the manipulation of people through different types of coercive media, or as a result of the enforcement of unjust laws. Some might even argue that man is flawed, that either his mind or his soul are corrupted, perhaps by something they may refer to as original sin. But few are willing to look deeply into that dark soul, and fewer still will even entertain the possibility that all external reality is the cause of an internal type of action that cannot be perceived by the physical senses or explained by rational science.

Even though it's happening right in front of all of us now, the average person finds it very difficult to understand how ethereal things like thoughts, ideas, and belief structures could possibly bring about great change. At best they might acknowledge that these highly ethereal things are important, but for them the fundamental catalyst of physical reality is physical action. They perceive this physical action when they witness wars, crimes, protests, and the rulership by dictators or by those they vote into political office.

As a result of what Alchemists have come to realize is an **imposed limitation on human awareness**, people are not able to perceive the more subtle internal energetic actions that now control them, nor the Alien intent that is behind this manipulation of the human world.

An Alchemist on the other hand is able to tune his or her perception, and as a result is able to clearly perceive these Internal Actions and Alien intent that shape human reality. This is so because for him or her, these seemingly ethereal things are not invisible suppositions, they are in fact quite real things that they can clearly identify and manipulate.

As a result of this greater perceptive ability, an Alchemist not only sees these energetic forms we call thoughts, ideas, and intent as they churn within the space around us, they can also look beyond that space and discover how many of these thoughts, ideas and intent are being projected from a distant mind that desires sustenance.

This of course is not just an Alchemist's purview, there are many people who can perceive the power of thought, and there are even those who can perceive or deduce that there is indeed an external Intent, a dark external force, manipulating the whole of humanity right now!

But why should the Alchemist's energetic view matter to you?

The energetic view matters not so much because it reveals something new, but because such a robust Cognitive Perspective shows Alchemists a way to fight against the negative external forces that now rule this planet.

Indeed, the fact that this planet is under the thumb of oppressive forces is something that has been known by some people for millennia, and there are some very good researchers who are sharing this information now in greater and greater numbers.

But what these researchers fail to provide to any great degree I believe, is a way to cancel out these negative external forces; a way to truly fight and overcome this dark control!

Why I write this book, and why I provide the Alchemist's energetic point of view here, is to not only provide a different and hopefully clearer picture of what is going on, but also to make available information that I find lacking through other sources.

As I read the information available on this subject, I have noticed that there is very little detail on how to confront and overcome these oppressive forces. Certainly there is some very good information about the particulars of what is being done to humanity, and as such the good advice always comes down to; realize what is going on, and fight against it by not taking part in the corruption. In other words, clear your mind and try to ignore it, and hopefully it will ignore you.

But as many have realized, not participating is no longer an option, because as I pointed out in Chapter 1; it is impossible for a person to avoid a meme that has become big enough. Quite simply, it is impossible to resist these Archonic forces by simply trying to ignore them, or for that matter through any type of external physical action. **The only possible way to fight and win this war is through the correct and constant use of INTERNAL MANIPULATION / ACTION.**

This book then is most importantly about how to truly fight this malevolent (from a human perspective) force, before the coming 'technological singularity' makes any large resistance impossible.

In order to do this, I find it necessary to reveal Alchemical methods that have hitherto been hidden behind jargon, metaphor and garble. I find the revelation of these techniques necessary because this is the only way to provide a logical framework for what is going on, what is most likely going to happen if this force continues unopposed, and most importantly how to succeed where so many others are now failing:

And that is to provide a structured and systemic methodology that can beat the Archonic forces that are currently consuming the human race.

With these Alchemical techniques at your disposal, it is my hope that you will not only be able to have a happier, fuller life, but also expand your freedom as an individual and your possibilities as a human being. From a larger perspective I hope that the use of these techniques will help in whatever small way to begin to turn the tide against the Great Archon and bring forth a new era in human development.

> It is indeed the case that these techniques and the information provided should allow you to do what many talk about wanting to do, or claim to do, but that don't seem to have a coherent and structured outline for;

which makes doing what they advocate very difficult.

It is my hope that this book will be similar to my 'Out of Body Experiences' book, in that it will provide a logical framework and a step by step procedural system for Alchemy.

But why Alchemy?

What is so special about this supposedly flawed attempt at chemistry?

Alchemy is the most misunderstood body of knowledge there is, and the reason for this, as I am trying to make apparent in this book, is directly related to the reasoning mind that now rules human perception. Alchemy is the beginning and the end (the Alpha and Omega) of all occult knowledge, and it represents in my opinion, the best (and perhaps only) way to both attain power and escape the predatory forces that now stand above humanity. It can show you how to recover the power that is being sucked out of you every second of every day, and how to

> use that power to better your world and escape imprisonment.

In order to give this methodology coherence, I have begun by providing a rationalistic view of our times and introduced the idea that this is but one Cognitive Stance based on one type of logic, which I refer to a mechanistic cause and effect logic.

I can now elaborate on the fact that there are indeed many different types of logic; the only difference between them is how they define causality. Contrary to what some might believe, modern science knows that this is so and quite openly practices different types of logic depending on which particular branch of science is being studied. Good scientists also know quite well that using different types of logic, changes the types of perception possible and unveils complete new worlds that function through the use of completely different laws, than the ones we are used to in our regular mundane worldview.

Perhaps the best example of an accepted yet wholly divergent logic can be seen in modern physics and computing.

For the most part, a great deal of physics and most computing is done using a type of logic referred to as mechanistic or Newtonian Logic. This logic defines the world through what to us might seem like a sane and common sense perspective because this logic seems to be almost hardwired into the human brain. This logic is based on a polarity paradigm where things are defined as either one thing or another within a duality:

- yes/no
- up/down
- black/white
- true/false
- on/off
- and in the regular computing world 0/1

This logic is common sense; it makes the complex understandable and seems to be both complete and coherent to the human mind. With it we have made amazing discoveries and created amazing machines; like the computer, which allow us to extend the power of this logic in order to calculate and accomplish tasks that would be impossible for the human mind alone.

Regular computers, like the one you have at home, use tiny on/off switches (called transistors) inside an integrated circuit that allows these transistors to carry out logical operations automatically. In this way they are able to use the laws of mechanical logic to figure out really hard problems.

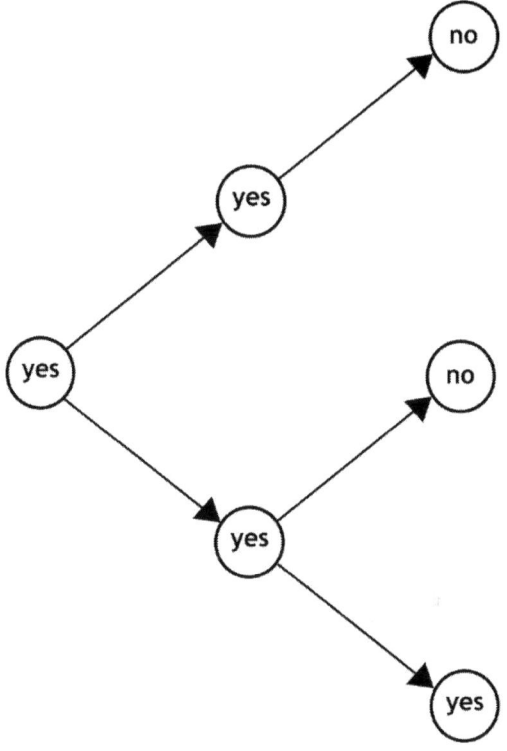

But this causal interpretation, even though it is a most powerful logic, cannot help us to understand or calculate some parts of the world using this circuit structure. It cannot help us to make sense of the infinitely small or the infinitely large for example, which are now becoming more and more relevant in human technological development.

As a result, scientists have been working on a different kind of logic which they refer to as Quantum Logic or Quantum Mechanics.

Quantum Logic is a very powerful and complex cause and effect model that can be used to explain things that seem almost magical to the human mind. I, for example, borrowed a great deal from this logical framework when I put together my book on Out of Body Experiences. I needed to do this because it is currently the only way to give coherence to experiences that defy Space and Time as we understand these terms.

Unlike regular logic and regular computational science that relies on polarity (0/1), the quantum model relies on a distributive law that encompasses multiple universe probabilities.

This sounds crazy and seems even more crazy when you realize that quantum computers are literally sealed cubes like something out of a horror movie, that are quite literally tapping into multiple universes to get answers to questions that are impossible to access and decipher any other way.

In order to better understand this, think of a Quantum computer as a computer made up of all these really tiny sealed boxes (which are in fact a new type of transistor), and inside every single one of these boxes is a poor cat that belongs to a scientist by the name of 'Schrodinger'. Every single one of these cats in every single one of these boxes, because of a random timer that controls the release of poison gas placed inside the boxes, can either be alive or dead depending on when you open the box.

This means that using mathematics, there is a particular point when this tiny cat in this tiny box is both alive and dead at the same time! And the act of opening the box and looking to see if the cat is alive or dead collapses one world view as you find out whether the cat is now, at that moment that you look inside, either alive or dead. So the act of witnessing it, of paying attention to it, creates a probable world and collapses others!

Unlike a regular computer that works by assigning yes or no (0 or 1), Quantum computers work by playing with complete other world probabilities. What is meant by this is that they don't just work on probability like we might understand it when we roll dice for example. They actually work by tapping into complete other world realities that are far beyond anything that we could calculate using any type of probability formula. They use a logic that uses multiple universes to determine whether something is true, false, or both true and false at the same time. This allows these computers to tackle massive problems since they are able access whole other world causality timelines.

Furthermore, these calculations cannot be witnessed while they are being performed by the computer because the act of looking at them, of perceiving these calculations by a human witness, collapses the probable world in which these calculations are taking place. If you look inside the box, you condemn the cat to either being alive or dead and therefore limit the calculations possible by the computer. In a very real sense, this type of computer seems like some kind of magical oracle that is literally tapping into other dimensions of existence for answers!

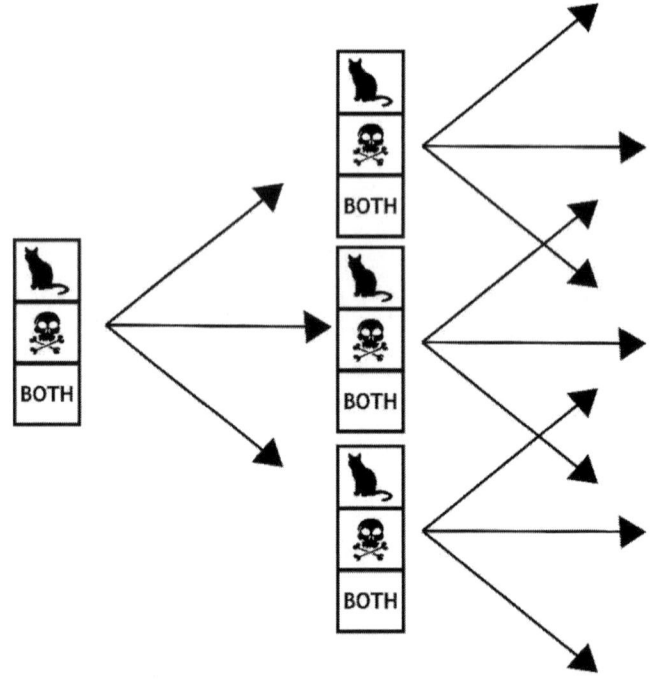

If you are still having trouble understanding all this, then do realize that even the best scientific minds of the time are still grappling with the perplexities of Quantum Mechanical Logic and the uses of a Quantum Computer.

This little foray into Quantum Logic is in no way something that you need to understand in order to apply the material in this book. I present it here in order to expose you to a whole new logic and a whole new world view that is being used right now by established scientists in an established field, so that you might get an idea of how legitimate and all-encompassing a different logical view can be.

A new logical view can completely alter the way a person perceives reality, and as a result, provides a totally different set of possibilities (or tools) that can be used to change the shape of reality.

The application of Quantum Logic in everyday human life is quite literally opening the door to a new cognitive position, a new reality, and it will change how humans see and acts upon this world.

The energetic view is also a different type of logic, and provides a different set of laws for cause and effect.

But unlike quantum logic which requires complex tools to use effectively, the Logic of the Energetic View can be used by a lone human being without any physical contraptions. The only thing required is the training and modulation of awareness.

In order to develop the ability to modulate your awareness so that you can begin to extend the power of your Will, of your Intent, it is necessary that I explain the Alchemical Trinity and how this relates to the power inherent within each of us.

CHAPTER 3
The Holy Trinity

URU AN-NA

When we look at ourselves in the mirror, we tend to see an object. Most of us are very fond of this object and learned long ago that this particular object is ourselves.

The Energetic Cognitive Position though does not see an object, it sees an assembly of aware energy that is in direct contact with all of the energy around it; it sees an infinitely small bubble floating inside an infinitely large sea of energy.

Since we tend to only see thick, seemingly stable matter when we see ourselves, we fail to realize that we are fundamentally energetic things that are in a constant state of give and take with the entirety of the world around us. All such interactions with this Energetic Sea in which we reside, in is the flux and flow of life and death, can be referred to as a Life Cycle.

Alchemists are very interested in the fluctuations that make up the human Life Cycle because energy is everything to an Alchemist. As such, they have devoted lifetimes to studying how the amount of energy available to a person changes that person, how energetic fluctuations happen, and what these fluctuations mean to a human being.

Such intricacies would require entire libraries to contain them all; fortunately there is no need to know such contemplations in great detail. What must be understood is that:

1. Energy is all important to Alchemists.

2. Fluctuations in energy movement are the natural consequence of existence, they are existence, and their cause can be attributed to two major sources that I will discuss shortly.

First though, we must examine why energy is so important, specifically why acquiring extra energy is so deeply important to an Alchemist.

Indeed, the acquisition and the storing of energy is the most important thing in the world to an Alchemist, and one could rightly state that a person cannot become an Alchemist unless they have managed to acquire and store enough extra energy.

This extra energy is very important because it acts like a type of evolutionary propellant; it is quite literally **a transmutive agent**. This transmutive agent helps an Alchemist in two basic ways:

1. The most important thing that this extra energy provides is the power of focus. It could be said that everything in the life of a human being, is directly related to his or her power to focus and maintain consciously directed attention.

Focus is the power that allows the mind to be directed in one direction for prolonged periods of time. This ability to focus the mind completely in one direction is what allows an Alchemist to change his or her Cognitive Position, and to maintain that change for as long as it is needed.

By changing his or her Cognitive Position, an Alchemist is able to perceive reality in a completely different way, or one could say that by changing his or her Cognitive Position an Alchemist can be part of other world realities. So essentially, they can change their reality by changing their point of attention using an incredibly powerful focus of attention that they have acquired as a result of their ability to obtain/ingest/pull-in and store energy.

2. The second thing that this extra energy provides is an extra thrust, or it is perhaps better to say an extra intensity, to the thoughts that an Alchemist can generate.

While it is the case that focus of attention can increase the intensity of thoughts through the medium of time, the ability to have and project extra energy within the body, is a fundamental aspect of Alchemical work, and it is the foundational principle of transmutation. When I speak about transmutation, I mean the ability to bring subjective experience into objective reality; the ability to change the vibratory state of things.

Extra energy therefore is the only reason why some people are successful at bringing thoughts to physical reality (manifesting), and others are not. Extra energy is the underlying catalyst of Alchemical transmutation.

The acquisition and conservation of energy is very important, because it allows an Alchemist to be able to change external reality through Internal Manipulation. Without this extra energy, it becomes impossible to maintain true self-awareness, because the true self (without this extra energy) is easily drowned beneath the many waves that batter against it as it makes its way through the Dark Sea.

These waves that batter against the self are experienced in different ways by different people. For those who are quite psychically sensitive, these waves can actually be felt as 'the push of the world' in the form of strong thoughts, emotions, opinions, and desires. For most of humanity though, these waves are the endless memetic battles that we wage against each other from birth until death, and as the quite physical obstacles of life that we all face as well, like natural disasters, predators, diseases, bad traffic, bad people, Murphy's Law, etc.

In other words, if you wish to become yourself, and if you wish to free yourself from the massive influence of all of the things around you, you need to have enough energy to steer your own course.

Now that we know a little of why energy is so important to an Alchemist, and to anyone interested in living a strong, free life, *we must look into what the two major causes of energetic fluctuations are.*

The knowledge of what causes energetic fluctuations is very important because it is these External Forces that impede or facilitate energetic acquisition and storage; these are the evolutionary forces that all Alchemists and all of humanity have to deal with.

The two major sources of energetic fluctuations are:

1. External Forces, or External Intent:

    These types of fluctuation could, I suppose, be considered 'natural' movements in that they are experienced by all existence within our small section of the Dark Sea. Like our great oceans here on Earth, the energetic sea (the

Dark Sea) moves, churns, and swirls like any great ocean. Storms and tsunamis that might happen at one end of that infinite sea affect the other, and generally there is a constant tide that moves all free-flowing energetic structures up, down, and all around.

Within the Dark Sea there are also currents that might seem quite 'un-natural' from our human perspective. These currents are created by very powerful living beings (megalithic alien life, from the human perspective) that affect large portions of the Dark Sea. The human race is at this time being battered by the currents from such a life form. This powerful Alien life creates currents within the Dark Sea through the sheer force of its Will/Intent. These waves then crash against the human race and change humanity from the inside out.

Resisting this Alien Current is of grave importance to Alchemists and it should be of grave importance to all human beings because this Alien force is a predatory force that robs humanity of energy. For those who are not aware of the existence of this titanic life form, and for those who have not developed their personal Will in any way, life is indeed like the life of a small bubble within a tempestuous Dark Sea.

2. Internal Intent, or Will Force:

This is the energetic movement that is caused by the individual human being. Each human being, each aware bubble as it makes its way through the Dark Sea, creates energetic currents within and around itself as it changes the focus of its attention.

These individual movements of energy always begin inside and move outward. When these energetic movements are inside the individual person's energetic body, which the average person might refer to as a subjective experience, this force is referred to as Will Power or Will Force.

When these movements are able to move outside the individual's body and begin to actually create a current out in the Dark Sea itself, this force is referred to as Intent. **It is Intent, which is created by Will Force, through the manipulation of attention, that changes reality.**

For most people, Will Force and Intent are very minor movements of energy, meaning that the energetic currents that the average person creates as an individual being is a hardly noticeable force. As a result, the average individual is just a rudderless form that is being pulled this way and that by unseen and unsuspected forces that are in almost complete charge of its destiny.

Some people on the other hand have managed (through illumination and hard work, or through natural talent) to learn how to increase and control the focus of their awareness. These people can sometimes exert a great deal of energetic movement in and around themselves. Such people are often referred to as great leaders, mystics, psychics, or miracle workers.

An alchemist tries very hard to be one of those rare human beings that can create a great deal of current within the Dark Sea. They strive to be one of these rare people not because they want to rule others or because they want to perform great miracles; they strive because they want to overcome all External Intent and free themselves from the forces that would steal their power and limit their possibilities.

In this book, I have made it my goal to teach you about the basics of Alchemy so that you too can develop your own Will Force and Intent. In this way, you will be able to fight against a human world and an Alien Intent bent on subjugating you. In this book, I strive to teach you how to develop your own powerful Will Force in the

same way that Alchemists do, so that you can beat External Intent through the mastery of Internal Manipulation.

Through Internal Manipulation you will be able to Transmute bad things and events into good things and favorable events. You will be able to live a stronger more energetic life, and you will develop the power to bend the Will Force of others, to change their minds, when there is no other way to escape negative memetic attacks.

Alchemists, after much study, concluded that all such fluctuations of energy, both internal and external, were very important. But they did further conclude that the ability to control and manipulate Will Force is the most important achievement that any individual human being could engage in.

This was a highly practical conclusion based on the belief that no tiny spec of a human being could ever hope to control the external Will of the Great Dark Sea, but an individual could certainly strive to control their own Will and perhaps even a tiny bit of the Dark Sea within close proximity to them, which is possible through the refinement of personal Will into Intent.

As such, they began a methodical study of how Internal Will and Intent work and how to increase this power.

Through rigorous effort, they were able to classify three major energetic polarities, which accounted for how a human beings moved energy and exerted their Will both inside and outside themselves.

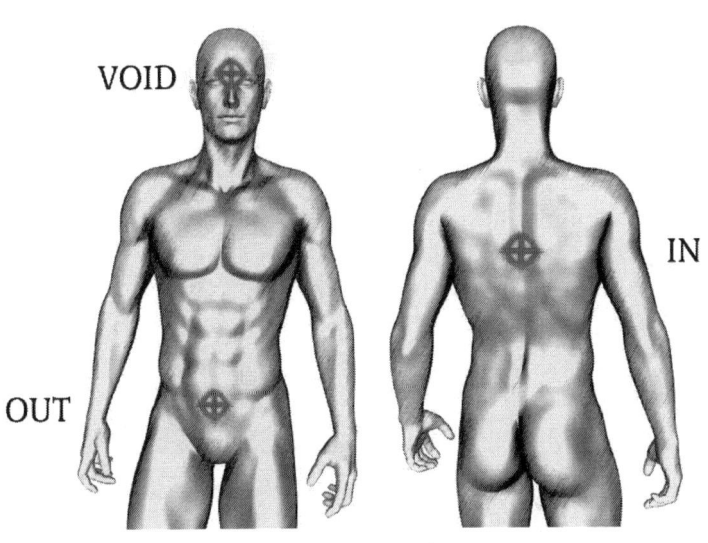

They found that a person fluctuated between these three major energetic polarities constantly, and this movement seemed to be a natural process that was a necessary aspect of being an alive, of being aware.

While I have named this TRIAD "In", "Out" and "Neutral/Void" in the diagram above for simplicities sake, it should be noted that these polarities are hard to define because they are greatly misunderstood aspect of the Life Cycle that have taken on many names and many mythic connotations. All this nomenclature and erroneous mythic allegory have made this 'Trinity' very difficult to understand.

Other names for the Holy Trinity include:

- light, energy, mass
- light, soul, body
- Father, Son, Holy Spirit
- purity, activity, inertia
- spirit self, outer expression, denser body
- spirit, mind, body
- positive, negative, void
- etc.

All these different names actually are examples of man trying to define and explain something that is most difficult to explain with words. This loss of perspective, brought about as a result of a restrictive Cognitive Position, is a theme that happens over and over again in the Alchemical world; an energetic truth is turned into an indecipherable description with little practical value thanks to the endless metaphor that the rational mind requires.

All this nomenclature and the endless mythical constituents that are attached to these named components of a simple and natural energetic movement/form, cloud true understanding. Quite simply, the TRIAD is a natural energetic fluctuation/form that is first and foremost an Internal Action, and then physically observable phenomena in the objective world. For example, a far better way to define the triad in objective terms is:

- in breath
- out breath
- in-between breath

From these three, the great firmament of existence is built, one breath cycle at a time.

Breath is everything; to stop the breathing cycle, the natural energetic cycle of life, is to die and return both form and consciousness back to the endless flow of the Dark Sea.

It is at this point that I find it prudent to introduce the concept of the 'Puffer':

Puffer is a word that true Alchemists use to describe those that try to practice Alchemy even though they have no real understanding of what Alchemy really is. A Puffer is a person who only knows about External Manipulation and therefore, tries to use external disciplines like chemistry or metallurgy to create a something that has no form as they might understand that term.

Since Puffers have no real understanding of Internal Manipulation, they are forever engaged in some odd laboratory work where they spend most of their time in front of some great furnace, 'puffing' air into it in order to get just the right temperature that they supposedly need, to 'chemistry' together a Philosophers Stone; which they of course believe is an actual stone.

True Alchemists though, are interested in Internal Manipulation only, so they know that the only real furnace is the one inside themselves. And the **Philosopher's Stone** is not an actual stone; it is **an energetic bundle that has been distilled through the manipulation of awareness, and intent.**

It is very important that you understand what is meant by 'Puffer', and how it is that the Puffer mentality has created objects and complexity where in actuality there is only natural law.

These misconceptions are most often not outright attempts at deception, but are actually the result of humanity being quite forcibly kept in a very limited Cognitive Position; in a very limited reality tunnel that makes people think that life is only a certain way.

I have discussed this limited reality tunnel already by stating that:

In order to manipulate his world, the average man, believing that he is an object surrounded by other objects, practices science and a type of limited logic, that is based solely on a mechanical interpretation of reality. This interpretation of reality posits that we are meat machines, surrounded by hard non-sentient things, and that it is only through reason that we can function effectively in the world. Life for the average man is cold, predictable, and full of limits.

Furthermore, I stated that Alchemists on the other hand believe that the world is actually one giant sea of energy, and that people are infinitely small self-aware bundles of energy within this grand sea. Since we are all energy, surrounded by energy, the only real difference between any one thing and any other is energy modulation. Human beings therefore, as self-aware bundles of energy, have the capacity to affect the energy within themselves and around them through that modulation of their personal energy/awareness. Alchemists accept as an energetic fact that the only real difference between any one human being and another is their ability to conserve and modulate their own energy; the more energy that a person has, the more that they can do. The Alchemist's interpretation of reality posits that human beings, and the seemingly hard objects around them, are far more malleable than it would appear. To an Alchemist, human beings are incredibly mysterious beings capable of outstanding things, and the world is a mysterious scary event that is quite literally beyond words.

As a result of this 'dumbing down' of human awareness, all energetic truths have been misinterpreted by people throughout our known human history. The knowledge of these energetic truths has been altered so deeply by humanity, that for the most part this information is no longer usable as an Alchemical methodology.

A Puffer for example, believes that Alchemy is about chemistry and that an actual cauldron is necessary in order to create the fabled Philosophers Stone. To real Alchemists though, the true cauldron is the human body, the energetic conglomeration of awareness that most people can only perceive as their physical being.

The true Philosopher's Stone is an energetic ball that is made up of both accumulated external energy and internal energy that is refined inside the human cauldron. This Stone is then used like a key to open up whole new worlds, worlds that the Alchemist can then perceive and interact with.

Imagine then the fallacy that is the study of modern alchemy by those that true Alchemists call Puffers. To a true Alchemist these people seem sadly insane, lost in a world where only External Manipulation seems possible.

The TRIAD or the Holy Alchemical Trinity, is another such energetic truth that has been altered by people like the Puffers, whether these people practice some sort of alchemy or not. Limited perceptions cannot conceive of power without measurable substance that affects man in ways that are beyond reason. As such, reason fights and threatens, and comes up with its own rules and designs that turn the unmeasurable into things that can then be ruled (think about that word 'rule' most carefully, it can mean that act of measuring and the act of lording over).

It is not my desire to lose myself in dogma and nomenclature because all such actions work towards the greater development and refinement of objective prisons. The naming and the desire to measure these forces using rules that the reasonable mind has created, in order to objectify the infinity that surrounds us, will only create barriers and cages that limit the possibilities of man the magical beast.

Let us then contemplate the Holy Alchemical Trinity using the most simplistic terms possible. It is my hope that using these simple terms and mechanisms, you will be able to see the direct correlation between the Internal (which is the simply the natural movement of a type of currently measureless energy) and the External as perceived by humanity (which is the physical act of breathing for example). So, from our external human perception, we can see and refer to this energetic act as:

- Breath IN
- Breath OUT
- The quiet moment in between Breath IN and Breath OUT

Each one of these energetic polarities within the human body is caused by a direct transference of energy, as it flows in and out, and as it replenishes the body's energetic makeup. From a completely objective (that is, rational) point of view, this physical movement represents the intake of oxygen, the distribution of oxygen throughout the body, and the expulsion of oxygen and other by-products. If we stop breathing we die, if we die we stop breathing.

From an energetic perspective, this Triad of action is not seen as the intake of tiny objects named oxygen, that can be measured and identified as such. From an energetic perspective, the physical action just described hides (or it might be better to say masks) an internal action, an energetic movement that can't be seen clearly using our human senses when these senses are being used in what we refer to as the 'normal' way.

From an energetic perspective, what is happening is that there is this subtle flow of energy that is entering the awareness bubble, replenishing it and strengthening is connection to the Dark Sea, and is then being expelled in a slightly distilled form. One could also say that **breathing is the Dark Sea flowing through the awareness bubble.**

The similarity between what I refer to as the energetic perspective and the objective perspective might seem almost identical when I try to describe the breathing cycle, but such similarities are only the result of me being hampered by the use of a language that was created solely to interact with physical objects. Our languages are amazing creations that make living within the human community not only tolerable but also quite pleasurable. Unfortunately, these languages suffer from many limitations and I therefore implore you to always be careful how you interpret what I am trying to reveal to you, because our language will naturally have you seeing solid objects and linear events even though such objects and events are quite literally an illusion.

As an example of the limits of the objective view and of language, we can contemplate those people who exist now in the world who can do some amazing things, seemingly with the power of breath alone. In the East, there are tales of Yogis and other mystics, some who have been carefully observed by scientists. Some of these mystics do not seem to require any food or water to live, and there are others for example that can generate body heat so that they do not require clothing in even the harshest temperatures.

Our limited senses tell us and our language describes, lungs as being these certain objects defined as body organs, and oxygen as this certain object that we breathe that is itself bound by laws neatly described in the periodic table of elements; what a remarkable description of the life process really!

But this description, as amazing as it is, creates a cage that says, "there is no way that a person can create food or heat from oxygen and lungs". Postulations are made about how there might be another object inside oxygen that we may have not classified yet that can account for how these people are making food, liquid, and heat from nothing. There are also theories about how perhaps certain human organs can be trained to do things that have not yet been discovered to be possible. But generally, any such postulations leads to very little because the cage created by language and rationality stop people from searching further, looking deeper. Insanity is the only thing that the rational mind can accept as a possibility, when it contemplates the likelihood that lungs and oxygen alone can create food and heat.

All of these speculations are of course a result of not being able to see humanity and the world around us for what it all really is: energy. If such gifted mystics keep popping up and more are studied, it might just happen that science will classify some new substance or discover that the pancreas can restore body fluids, but really all such theory vindication will be actual proof of humanity's ability to manifest new probabilities within a rational world view, and not that the objectification of the world is somehow the best way to perceive, classify, and conceive reality.

But the rationalist majority should not worry about such things. Since the classification of the objective world is now supposedly quite complete (that is, science does not believe that there is much left to discover on this Earth). The human mind, within the bounds of its rational stance, will take it for granted that all such seeming miracles are the result of delusion, because no sane (aka rational) person could possibly believe that there are those who don't have to eat anymore. Lord knows, using life force to heal others, create heat, create thought forms, manifest objects, etc. are all delusions of people who just don't really have the capacity to know how the world really works.

This is the Puffer's curse, the curse of the rationalist perspective. This perspective helped to bring about chemistry and it also helped to establish some of the methodology that would be used in other sciences. I, and many of you I am sure, am very grateful for the endless things that science has given humankind, but as it has helped humanity and changed the face of this planet, it has also helped to bind our potential and taken away much of the magic that we now so desperately need if in order to escape our current predicament.

So, let us now forget this rationalist mind for a little while, this Puffer's curse that would turn a magical being into a caged fool, huddled over beakers and stoves, and let us contemplate The Holy Trinity with an unbound mind.

CHAPTER 4
The Power of the IN Polarity

I have been throwing a number of different terms at you, different nomenclature and methodologies that Alchemists use to classify and work with energy. I have also stated that such classifications can be quite misleading because they tend to reinforce a perceptive view that would classify the world as a hard, object filled place. I also stated that this objective view can cause all sorts of difficulties when it comes to actually applying these energetic principles because even though our language is good at objectification, it is sorely lacking when it comes to describing subjective action.

Unfortunately, there is no way around this language problem because there really is no other way to communicate this information to you. I think that if you keep in mind the fact that we are dealing with energy, instead of objects, and that these energetic 'forms' are not bound by space and time as we understand those terms, your understanding and your ability to use these techniques will not be so hampered by my words.

That being said, let us continue with our study of the Holy Trinity as it is understood and practiced in the Alchemical tradition.

When it comes to the Holy Trinity of Alchemy, the most important aspect within its functional application is the necessity to master the principals of:

BALANCE

Just like anything in our lives, if things are maintained in balance then stability is achieved. This stability means that there is a less random and chaotic flow of energy: **nothing is more important than any other thing so all things flow in an ordered and impeccable way.**

If *dis-balance* happens, balancing forces will present themselves that will naturally, but sometimes quite brutally correct this dis-balance. This means that dis-balance destroys orderly impeccability and the resulting anarchy that is created from this dis-balance, acts as an oftentimes painful balancing force that will eventually bring order to any energetic system.

An Alchemist seeks balance as the most harmonious and desired state of being possible. But he or she sometimes seeks dis-balance as well because as an energy manipulator, dis-balance is the most natural way to achieve strong energetic action.

This means that no one particular polarity within the Holy Trinity is more important than any of the others. It is the case though, that at every single moment in time (whether you are measuring time in seconds or eons) any one particular polarity of the Trinity can play a bigger role than the others. Quite simply, there is a time for breathing IN (which means there is a time when it is most important to draw in energy), there is a time for breathing OUT (which means that there is also a time for pushing energy out, or extending one's Will), and there is time for holding still in VOID (which means there is a time for the absolution of time, through the complete cancellation of thought and energy flow).

When the Holy Trinity was taught to a novice in the art of Alchemy, it was always considered best to start with the VOID polarity because this was the one polarity that most clearly revealed the illusory and the highly distorted nature of this world, as it is perceived by the average person.

So instead of learning how to or extend one's Will or to pull IN energy, a student of Alchemy was usually taught the energetic way by first learning how to attain energetic stasis. This stasis meant the complete quietude of thought, or to put it in other words; the complete stopping of any and all energetic movement within the body, within the energetic conglomeration that makes up a human being.

This training was often a very long and laborious affair that could take a lifetime depending on the capabilities of the student.

This task, of achieving energetic stasis, was often taught to the neophyte by having him or her learn about the power of attention. A number of exercises were used for this purpose, such as the act of staring at a dot on a wall or having him or her perform some tedious task that required their complete attention. These exercises were continued for years and were usually supplemented with other teachings meant to impart the energetic truth of reality. The neophyte was also forced to take part in a number of different responsibilities and ceremonies that were designed to make them question everything that they thought they knew about the world around them.

The final outcome, after many years of work usually, was a person who could completely stop their energetic flow, which was often referred to as stopping all thought, or attaining VOID.

Attaining VOID, as you might suspect, created great dis-balance within the neophyte's energetic body. This dis-balance meant that a vacuum was created within the body that allowed this person to perform amazing energetic feats such as, travelling through space and time or achieving the much-coveted ability to see the world from an energetic perspective.

After this first polarity was mastered, the now initiated Alchemist would be taught IN, that is the pulling in of energy.

Through a great deal of Out of Body work, or *energetic scouting* as I call it, I have come to the conclusion that such neophyte beginnings are a thing of the past; something to be practiced in a time when there were less people on this Earth, a time when that external Alien Intent seemed to have far less power. Now with billions of minds all reflecting that malevolent (from the human perspective) external Intent, it is no longer feasible to try and start from the

VOID, in my opinion. It is my belief that the only way to begin the Alchemical process of energetic mastery, is to first and foremost learn how to fight the negativity that seems to be so prevalent in these modern times. By starting the Alchemical journey from the IN polarity, I believe that it is not only possible to attain mastery, but also to actually thrive in these dark times.

In my previous book, *The Vampire's Way to Psychic Self-Defense*, I gave a detailed description of how the mastery of this IN Tri-polarity could be used to protect yourself from human negativity, and from the energetic predation by the non-organic predatory lifeforms that are so prevalent now.

Since it is my desire to make this an all-inclusive book, meaning that I wish to provide a complete work that can stand alone without the reader having to read my other books, I will break down the basics of this IN Tri-polarity here. If you have read my previous book mentioned above, then I hope that this information will help clarify even further what the manipulation of this first energetic position means, and how it can be used in order to acquire energy so that you can thrive in an environment where so many others are crashing and failing.

It is indeed the case that we seem to be surrounded on all sides by negativity. You can't turn on the television, go on the Internet, or even talk to a friend without being flooded by negative energy. This negativity floods our lives and does its best to put us in a negative mental states and situations, that then cause us to experience even more negativity.

It is also the case that our increasing population makes it nearly impossible to find solitude and stability. Everywhere you look, wherever you go, there is always somebody there, and it is quite often the case that those you do find there do not have your best interests in mind.

But contrary to what most might believe, it is not negativity that is really the problem, the real problem is excessive energetic flares!

Whenever you have a really intense emotional outburst, whether it is classified as being negative— OR POSITIVE—by you, what is really going on is that your body is having a powerful reaction to some kind of stimulus. This stimulus causes a great deal of energetic build up in you, which is then released into the environment either like a giant flash or a simmering ebb.

An energetic flare then, is an emotion. It is intense emotional outbursts of any kinds.

And it is this energetic outburst that this Alien Force is after. This is the distillation of energy that the Great Archon needs for food!

As I mentioned earlier, this world has become a world of belief structures, all competing in this seemingly gigantic evolutionary battle in which supposedly one belief will become top banana. Ours is a world of propaganda, where we are in a constant state of struggle as we adopt certain beliefs, or memes, and then go about trying to force these beliefs on others.

Have you ever wondered why this is so? Science would say that this competition of the memes over our minds is just the natural result of evolution, caused by the next level of competition within a group of organisms that have attained self-awareness. But some might wonder, is this the only way to evolve? And if you think about it, can it really be said that humanity has evolved very much from a spiritual perspective, from this great meme battle?

There is a great force Out There, a megalithic Alien Presence that has hijacked human awareness and has almost completely halted humanity's slow march towards greater enlightenment and true freedom. It has done this by projecting its Intent upon our minds with such force that humanity now believes itself to be this screwed up evil thing that has to destroy to create.

One powerful meme tells us that we are evil, gross, sick, fallen children detached from nature. Another tells us that we are natural predators within a harsh world and that we must destroy in order to survive. From these two powerful memes we create tempest upon tempest of dark emotion which serve no human on this planet, it only causes more and more strife as we fight and worry about a life that seems to be endless struggle and contradiction. And when we are not lost in all this negativity, we lose ourselves in memes that speak of endless love, compassion, and peace, so that we then give up whatever energy we might have left in the form of waves of love for our planet and our fellow man, because as this meme tells us; love and happiness are the answer to everything.

All of these memes do one basic thing, and that is to cause energetic flares that this Alien Force then consumes!

These memes do not really help us evolve in a marked way and they certainly will not allow us to discover a utopia where humanity finally finds peace and enlightenment. These memes are aberrations placed before us, clouding our perceptions and forcing us to discharge huge sums of energy in the form of useless emotions. These emotional outbursts, which are pure distilled energy, are consumed by this Alien force like a man squeezing a ripe peach in order to drink the nectar inside.

Please note that I am not saying that all emotions are bad, what I am saying is that the vast sum of emotional outbursts are the result of thoughts and ideas that are not our own, and that these emotional indulgences serve no real purpose except to feed a megalithic force that owns us in the same way that we might own cows in a field.

But there is a way to fight these memes.

The great benefit of the IN Tri-polarity is that it provides a way for us to fight against this eternal battle for our minds by giving us a way to not only deal with this negativity, but also a way to thrive within it. This is so because the IN Tri-polarity concerns itself with the absorption of energy; it is that energetic state where the human awareness bundle opens itself up to the Dark Sea and actively sucks IN the energy all around it, in order to feed itself and gain more energy in order to extend life and power.

If you know anything about the yogic practice of pranayama, the Chinese practice of chi-kung, or even the incredibly fascinating trend of the Vampiric awakening that is taking hold of the Western world, then you will know a little bit, or a lot, about the absorption of life force from the environment.

All these methodologies concern themselves, to a greater or lesser degree, with the active intake of life force from the world around us using different techniques, that when they are examined closely, seem to be almost identical to each other. While each of these methodologies might propose a different ideological tangent, they all work using very similar techniques that employ breath, visualization, and internal pumps that absorb external energy and provide vitality and health to those who practice it.

Certainly, pranayama and chi-kung are complete energetic systems, while the Vampiric methodology that is growing in the West combines aspects of both these systems and introduces new ones based on a more predatory ideal.

What I find most interesting though is that all these energetic systems for the most part tend to only deal with what could be considered positive energy, or what some might call the 'natural' energy that surrounds all life. Even in advanced levels in pranayama and chi Kung, and even in Vampiric techniques that teach a type of predatory psychic vampirism, there is very little mention of how to accumulate energy that is most often referred to as 'negative'. What I mean by this is that these systems seem to solely be based on the idea that positive or natural energy is the only kind of energy available for psychic ingestion.

Again, you might think that perhaps within the techniques employed by Psychic Vampires for example, there would be some kind of methodology that allows a person to gain vitality, that is gain energy, from the negativity all around them, but this is not 'generally' the case. Energy vampires are usually interested in ingesting energy from willing hosts or perhaps ingesting energy from within large crowds that are generally projecting positive energy. We all seek beauty and pleasure I suppose, even Vampires, and we all move away from pain, suffering and evil.

The thing is though that, **there is no such thing as negative or positive energy; there is only energy!**

As such, I am afraid that I cannot consider any of these energetic systems complete from the Alchemical perspective because their understanding of energy seems to have limited connotations which, again seem to be the result of language and our objectification and classification system.

For an Alchemist, the IN Tri-polarity does not concern itself with ingesting what could be termed positive energy, which is a certain subjective classification of energy only. Alchemy involves itself in the ingestion of ALL energy, and specifically targets what might be termed negative energy because there is so much of it around.

This IN Tri-polarity then becomes an incredible powerful source of power, especially in these new times. This is so because the mastery of this Tri-polarity can allow a person to gain great power by feeding on the most prevalent energy available: negative energy.

Why is this so important?

And how does this relate to the active fighting-off of this negative Intent that now rules the world?

The IN Tri-polarity is infinitely important because by learning how to use this Tri-polarity, we can essentially consume that negative energy and Intent that is now clouding human perception, and with it we can do something outrageous:

Instead of being manipulated by this negative Intent, we can feed on it!

We can also feed on all of the negativity that this negative intent is causing on this planet. The IN Tri-polarity allows us to feed on our mind, which isn't totally our mind but the projection of a foreign evil, and moreover we can feed on all the negativity that this foreign Alien force is causing on this planet!

Think about the possibility of being able to gain massive amounts of energy from your enemy, so that the more that it/he/she pushes against you, the more that you are able to gain power from that push.

Hate, pain, evil, worry, sorrow, fear, delirious and indulgent love, blind compassion, then become food; a never-ending energy source that an Alchemist can use for his or her own evolution.

Within the context of our regular lives, the ability to absorb negativity has incredible potential. Any time someone tries to push their beliefs on you, or tries to fill your mind with the thoughts that are engendered by any indulgent belief structure, what these people are doing is using all of the personal energy that is available to them to create/project their thoughts and feelings upon you and the world at large. Their

Will/Intent in the form of thoughts and ideas, acquires form as a result of the amount of emotion that these people generate, and then this energetic form is projected at the environment around them; and at you specifically.

That is the power of awareness, the ability to give life, to manifest, to remold energy into different forms; quite simply the ability to refine energy within the awareness body and output that refined energy into the environment. Human beings are natural, and quite powerful, energy distillation systems; they are creators.

Unfortunately, this power is being appropriated by a life form determined to use this power to feed itself.

So, what we have is Alien Intent, an external force that is projecting energy into the human world from a dimension that is currently outside of the perceptive range of the average person. This energy, that has been given direction and purpose thanks to that Alien Intent, changes the perceptive capabilities of all the human beings that it touches and then forces humanity (who are a large collective of self-aware life forms) to refine this Alien Energy along with whatever bit of energy that they might possess themselves. This Alien Life then descends upon this collective human awareness pool and sucks up the energy that humanity has refined.

You can think of this sort of like distillation: you put a certain compound through a certain distilling mechanism and at the other end you are rewarded with a perfected new substance that you can then ingest. It is Alchemy in titanic proportions!

Unfortunately, this distillation of energy from the human collective is not a benign thing. This process, which I call 'distillation' in order to explain it in the most human way possible, is very costly to humanity because it drains humanity not only of the energy that is provided by the Alien Intent, but also of the inherent energy that is inside every human being. This inherent human energy, which at one time allowed us all to be incredibly powerful magical beings, is now food for a type of life form that cares for us in the same way that we might care about the chickens that we stick in tiny cages for the entirety of their lives to consume at our leisure.

Poetic justice or not, I think that we would all agree that escaping this cage is in the best interest of all humanity.

The mastery of the first Tri-polarity stops this energetic distillation of humanity by teaching a person how to absorb this energy that has been given negative (from the human perspective) purpose by Alien Intent. It quite literally shows the adept how to feed off of this Alien Parasite, completely turning the tables on monstrosities that would turn humanity into a food source.

In order to understand how this is possible, it is best to think of a person as being like a magnet. A human being has the potential, by focusing on this IN polarity, to turn him or herself into a type of magnet that draws in energy into itself.

As I have said, this sucking in of energy happens quite naturally without any need for human intervention. A person can and does absorb energy in the most natural way throughout his or her life, in the same way that a person quite naturally has the necessity to breathe IN. The thing is though, that such automatic, or autonomic to be more precise, functioning does not allow for the refinement of this skill, and the refinement of this skill is of paramount importance as you now know.

Exercise: Energy Absorption Technique

In order to perform this IN drawing of energy in a more conscious way, begin by finding a quiet place where you can be alone for about 15 minutes. Later, do this in crowded places, negative places, or whenever you feel any large distasteful energy wave or flare either inside or outside of yourself:

- Stand with your feet shoulder width apart and try to relax your body as much as possible.

  It is very important that you relax your body as much as possible because the ability to sense energy and the ability to move this energy throughout your body becomes much easier the more that you are able to relax. Relaxation of the body can be a very simple process if you treat it as a fun game and don't take it too seriously. It then just becomes a matter of focusing your attention on the desire to become more and more relaxed, to the point that your body feels so relaxed that it's about to collapse.

- If you feel that a certain part of your body, like your shoulders perhaps, is still tense, then focus your attention on that area and tell yourself to relax, focus your attention on the desire to relax this part of your body, and perhaps say to yourself, "relax".

- Once you feel that you are in a relaxed state, I want you to pay attention to the world around you. Focus your attention on all the objects around you, whether you are in a room or outside somewhere in nature. Think about the ground beneath you and the sky above you. Try to see and feel yourself as being just a tiny single entity in the middle of great big world, and then use your imagination to feel that you are becoming one with this world.

- When you think that you can almost sense the entirety of this world within you, I want you to breathe IN. Try to make this breath IN the slowest breath that you have ever done, so that it perhaps takes you 10 seconds to half a minute to breathe IN completely.

- As you breathe IN, I want you to imagine that you are pulling in energy from all of the things around you, imagine seeing and feeling this energy come to you and into you. Imagine that the entire world, the entirety of that world that you had been feeling, has within it an essence, an internal spirit energy, that you are now drawing into yourself through the power of your very slow IN breath.

- Imagine that as you are breathing IN this very slow breath, and as you pull the energetic essence from all the things around you, that this essence is being absorbed by your body; it is being sucked in by the very pores of your body. Your entire body has become like a magnet (or if you like, your body has become like a great vacuum) that is now drawing into itself all of this energetic essence.

- As your body pulls into itself all of the energetic essence from everything around it, this essence is being pooled in the very center of your body. This energy that you have absorbed pools like a large glowing ball at the very center of your being that grows in intensity, power, and brightness as you absorb more and more energy.

- When you feel like you just can't breathe in anymore because your lungs are full, I want to hold your breath for 5 seconds. As you hold your breath, try to feel this ball of energy at the center of your being, around the area where you imagine your stomach to be. And as you feel this ball of energy, try to visualize it becoming more and more concentrated.

- Then while still holding your breath, imagine that the energy contained within this glowing sphere of power begins to spread throughout your entire body filling it with vitality and strength.

- After these 5 seconds, or however long you think it's necessary, I want you to breathe out in a nice relaxing sigh. What I mean by this is that I want you to just let go of all the tension that your body might have accumulated as you were pulling energy into yourself, and as you relax your body, I want you to release the air inside your lungs by letting this air come out of you in the most natural way possible. This most natural out breath will be just like a relaxing sigh. You know that you are doing it right when you actually feel like you left something inside you after this sigh; like you have ingested a small but clean and powerful meal.

- Once this relaxing out breath sigh is complete, I want you to once again begin to breathe IN. Repeat the same process as before by breathing IN as slowly as possible and as you do so, once again imagining that you are pulling into yourself, that you are sucking up into yourself, the energetic essence from everything around you.

- Continue this energetic process for a count of at least five IN breaths. Once you are done I think you will be incredibly surprised at how much more vital you will feel.

This technique will allow you to absorb energy anywhere and will allow you to greatly increase the kind of vitality that you feel. It is through the mastery of this technique that certain masters are able to go without food for extended periods of time, and how some of these masters are actually able to stop eating all together.

Such mastery though can take years, so please do not engage in any kind of fasting without talking to your doctor first, and always make sure that you have a qualified person assisting you.

When I teach this technique to people, usually the biggest problem I find is trying to explain to them what and how it is that we pull energy into ourselves. A person can sometimes have difficulty feeling the energy that surrounds them, and they have difficulty pulling or sucking this energy into themselves as a result of this lack of 'feeling sense'.

For this reason, I usually have them practice an exercise that I have mentioned in other books, but it is one which I find incredibly powerful at showing people how to move psychic energy into and out of themselves.

Exercise: Discovering and Using Your Psychic Energy Pumps

- As before, I recommend that you find a nice quiet room in your house, preferably a room that has some kind of table in it where you can place a cup or some other small object.
- Next, I advise people to try as hard as possible to pull the object that they placed on that table with only the power of their mind. Pretend that you are a Jedi Knight for example, or some kind of magical being that has telekinetic

powers, and try to pull that object to yourself with just the power of your mind.

- Now, I don't expect that you will be able to move this object with the power of your mind, but this exercise is very good at showing you the kind of energetic pull that you need to use in order to suck in energy into yourself. This is the pulling IN feeling that is most difficult to describe in words but that can be felt/sensed by performing this exercise.

One can think of it like some kind of internal pump that is pulling an external essence into itself, it is a sucking force that draws with varying intensity that which is outside of itself. It is this feeling that you must use when you are performing the breathing IN exercise above. I would therefore suggest that you practice this exercise of trying to pull IN an object and keep practicing it until you master that feeling. If you ever find that you are having trouble using your IN Tri-polarity technique, I would recommend that you go back to this exercise because it is, in my opinion, the most powerful way to teach you how to develop a very powerful energy pump.

This is the foundational exercise and the basic core for the IN Tri-polarity.

As we progress in this book, I will be introducing new topics and information that will allow you to refine your techniques. I will also detail how this ability can be used to fight against the negativity around us, and how to use it to turn the tables on the predator that now consumes most of humanity in a ruthless fashion.

As the book progresses I also hope to stress how interconnected the Tri-polarities are, and how this connection means that one cannot function properly without the others.

CHAPTER 5

Into the VOID

It's better to burn out than to fade away
NEIL YOUNG

If you will remember the diagram in Chapter 3, you will note that while all the polarities are separated they are nevertheless connected within our body, and like any well-functioning whole, all three must work together or else there will be dis-balance. No one polarity can become more powerful than the others or else energy will accumulate in excess in one aspect of the human psyche, of the human energetic soul, which will then dis-balance the others.

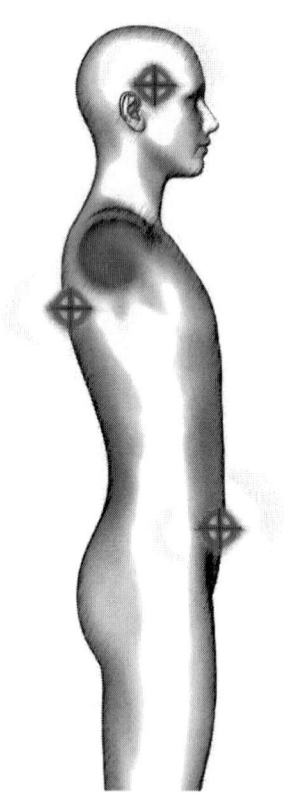

It is the case then, that in order to find balance we must NOT ONLY look into the IN Tri-polarity, we must endeavor to become masters of all three.

As I mentioned earlier, the polarity that is usually taught first is the VOID polarity. I have reversed the order in this book though, because I believe that this is the only possible way to teach the Holy Alchemical Trinity in these frenetic modern times.

This does not mean that the VOID polarity is not important, it is indeed very important because it is the one polarity that teaches us how to save the energy that we now have, which allows us to move unhindered within this world that would drain the life from the marrow of our souls. It is also the polarity that allows us to move beyond this world into other dimensions of existence; it is the magical doorway to other worlds.

To master the VOID Tri-polarity is to:

- master the ability to seal the energetic holes of the body
- to empty the boat
- to stop the mind
- to stop the world
- to attain Samadhi
- to attain satori
- to become aware of the Here and Now event
- go with the eternal flow of the now
- attain Forrest Gump like perfection

And through this polarity it is possible to:

- have Out of Body Experiences
- become a dreamer
- lucid dream
- travel to other dimensions and probable worlds

- attain complete enlightenment

If one or many of these descriptions sound familiar to you then you are probably someone who knows about Mysticism, most likely of the Eastern variety. The VOID Tri-polarity has become an incredibly powerful motif in Eastern religious and mystical thought, and these religious ideals and techniques are certainly a great resource for those interested in pursuing every possible detail of a life lived in pursuit of the VOID.

From an Alchemical perspective though, the most important way to describe this one point in the Holy Trinity is to say that it is the one polarity that shows you how to seal the energetic holes of the body. In this polarity, mastery of the human energetic body is achieved by controlling all the energetic flow IN and OUT of the body; it teaches the neophyte to actually stop all energetic flow, period. It is no more and no less than this.

Alchemy is first and foremost a practical system interested in energetic manipulation and not in mental floss, religion, symbology, politics, or definitions galore; something that I must admit is perhaps hard to believe when you read alchemy textbooks written by Puffers.

One can imagine how powerful the mastery of this one polarity could be, and indeed it was perhaps one of the most powerful mystical movements to ever overtake this planet. And to this day it is considered by some non-alchemists to be the only real form of self-enlightenment and freedom available to man.

It is the East that has excelled in the mastery of this VOID polarity in my opinion. And this one polarity alone has given birth to many mystical orders and religions such as Zen, Chan, Taoism, Buddhism, etc.

All these religious and mystical movements (except Taoism and Tantra perhaps) tend to focus almost completely on this one polarity and tend to consider the other two polarities within the Tri-polarity to be unnatural. Indeed some go even as far as calling any work done with the other two polarities evil; the work of the left hand path.

This is a mistake and a prejudice born out of ideological nomenclature and classification by the ego. Energy manipulation is not evil, in the same way that the use of electricity is not evil. Evil is born from the hearts of men and the influence of the Great Archon.

The conscious ego is an addition to the natural human mind, it was created by Alien intent. An aspect of this conscious ego has a great need to classify and categorize things as either good or bad.

But if some might want to push the issue, one could make the point that even the energy manipulation that some of these mystical schools engage in is bad because to stop all energy flow permanently, by focusing all efforts on just the VOID polarity, can permanently disable parts of the human psyche that need to be expanded, not destroyed.

Nirvana, which can be said to be the complete sensation of all energetic movement in the body (a state of being-non-being that many of these Eastern schools pursue at all costs), causes a complete implosion of the psyche. And while some believe that this implosion begets a passage into a new and better location within the Dark Sea that is beyond ego existence, I would personally not take any chances and test that theory, because all I see when I study such acts is total oblivion.

The Will/Intent of any one particular self-aware being can be classified as being either good or bad from the human perspective, but again, such classifications don't really apply from an energetic point of view. We humans for example, could classify the Alien Intent that is currently feasting on us as evil, but is it really evil? Or is it that our egos cannot handle the fact that another life form is treating us in the same way that we treat the other life forms on this planet?

There is no evil, there is only energy, and all those things that we classify as evil are actually our allies, because they are the challenges that push us to evolve.

Regrettably, the school of emptying the boat, sealing the holes, going with the now, and all the systems that advocate a type of 'self-obliterating' Nirvana, are incomplete by themselves, and can no longer save us from the predatory Alien Intent because that predatory Intent has become far too powerful in this modern time. The strain on us humans right now is unbelievably strong.

It is no longer possible to escape the powerful intent that now holds this world, by just trying to master the VOID polarity alone.

Have you ever wondered why it has become so common to hear about the great guru, or that saintly person, that goes from one day being the epitome of grace and goodness, to performing some terrible deed the next day? Why is it that those who climb so high can still fall so far?

The reason for this, is the fact that unless you are a COMPLETE master of the VOID polarity, which then posits that you have attained true and real Samadhi (true and complete 'enlightenment'), that Alien Intent will one day, sooner or later, find a crack in your focus of attention. And when this happens, this person will be plunged into a dark place, full of something terrible where before there was nothing at all; that could have them feel a previously unfelt emotion or impulse that could 'make' them commit the most heinous deeds possible.

In order to explain this further, I have to show you what mastery of the VOID polarity is.

Mastery of the VOID Tri-polarity concerns itself with halting all energetic flow. This means that there is no energetic flux from the Dark Sea that can affect the practitioner, which is no small feat to say the least, and there is no energetic leak from the practitioner's energetic body into the Dark Sea either.

When a master of this polarity attains Nirvana, which could be said to be the highest attainment within the bounds of this VOID polarity, he or she becomes a dark void within an already Dark Sea.

I know that many will disagree with this definition of Nirvana or Samadhi, and I feel that such objections are indeed quite legitimate and understandable. This disagreement though is, I believe, due to the problems with definitions and objectification that can't be avoided using language.

Many would say that Nirvana is achieved when one attains 'no-self', the realization of Brahman, and the end of the karmic cycle. Some might then presuppose that 'no-self' is different from 'no-thought', and that none of this has anything to do with total Energetic Containment.

Alchemists though, are solely interested in the energetic view, as this has proven itself time and again to be the most correct view possible. As such, it must be realized that the only way for no-self to exist is through the stoppage of all thought. Or one could say that the stoppage of all thought nullifies self. Moreover, it must be understood that this nullification of all thought can be extended or diminished; that is there can be varying degrees of no-thought.

But to whatever degree no-thought is achieved, it can only be achieved through the control of energetic flow; therefore no-thought is just one degree of Energetic Containment.

We could say for example, that all conscious thought could be stopped, which then opens up the labyrinth that is the subconscious, and allows one to access the seemingly near infinite power that is contained there.

And beyond that there is the possibility of attaining TOTAL nothingness, that is: no conscious thought or subconscious awareness, which is achievable by a select and powerful few. This total nothing would turn off all of the thoughts in the subconscious part of the psyche as well. Once this complete silence is achieved one begins to perceive true VOID; true darkness, or 'lightlessness' if you prefer. But even here one sometimes is able to perceive certain sensations, if the energetic currents from the Dark Sea are strong enough.

So then, one could master even these currents and completely VOID all energetic flux to finally attain true silence. This is truly Nirvana and all things are VOID. The word Nirvana means 'blow out' and indeed a person who attains this kind of incredible mastery over this polarity has blown him or herself out from this existence.

If we contemplate the progression of quietude, as a neophyte becomes a great master, we can see how definitions might seem different depending on how much quietude is achieved. It is perhaps the case that some might believe that 'no-conscious-thought' is enough, while others might find that no-self cannot possibly be achieved until all thought and sensation are voided completely. And yet others might have a different interpretation of what Nirvana is or what voiding the karmic cycle might entail, depending on their ideals and their definitions of all of the terms that they use.

From an Alchemical perspective, all such definitions are essentially irrelevant. What is relevant is that all no-thought or no-self or whatever else, can only be achieved when Energetic Containment is mastered to one degree or another. For an Alchemist, the VOID polarity is all about Energetic Containment:

- thoughts are a projection of energy; to stop thoughts you must stop or contain this energetic projection, therefore 'no-thought' is Energetic Containment.
- the actualization of self, either through thought, sensation, will, intent, desire, etc. is a projection of energy. The self, the act of being, is a projection of energy, therefore stopping this being's existence, to whatever degree, is: Energetic Containment.

Nothing matters in the VOID Tri-polarity but Energetic Containment.

So why do so many holy men and women fall? And why are so many falling now?

They fall because their mastery of Energetic Containment is not perfect, and I would argue that unless you are a master that has 'blown him or herself out' through Nirvana, which I would argue is dying through energetic implosion, Energetic Containment alone will never be enough to withstand the Alien Intent that rules our planet.

This is not to say that all these people should be better masters, or that complete Energetic Containment is the only real way, and that everything else is wrong. As I have said, words are a most inappropriate way to describe energetic truths. I feel that it is always best to use the most simple and concise terms possible when trying to describe these principles and techniques. In this way a person can begin to practice these techniques quickly and efficiently, and discover the complexities of the energetic universe that I refer to as the Dark Sea, through direct body experiences instead of words.

Language will always get us in trouble in the end; it will shut doors and it will build giant objective barriers where such barriers and limitations do not exist.

Simply then, Energetic Containment, or the mastery of the VOID Tri-polarity alone, is not enough to deal with the Alien Intent that now controls this world. Neither of the three Tri-polarities by themselves are enough to deal with this most grave problem. And unfortunately, it is nearly always the case that these polarities are taught as separate things, each by itself and completely ignoring or disavowing the other two.

Some might say, "VOID is good, it is the way, it does not PUSH OUT on others and it does not PULL IN and take from the world either. It is beyond forceful expression of will (which is sickness) and it does not desire from the world (which is sickness) either, it is the only way to perfect Dharma."

Others say, "IN is best, it takes like the world takes, all is predation and it is best to be the top predator. Be the best taker that you can be, only then will you find immortality."

Still others say, "OUT is the only one that is best, you must put your will and intent out there. You must constantly think what you want, always knowing what you don't want so that you can focus on what you do want, always pushing, always being your best, always thinking of God, always being the happiest, the most loving. Always project goodness, always practice love, the golden rule; to get the world you want, you must create it one thought at a time."

Each one of these represents an ideology, a religion, a way of being. And each one is but one polarity in a Holy Trinity that cannot exist without the others. To overemphasize one at the cost of the others is to create a dis-balance that will only bring ruin in the long run if not managed properly. In Alchemy balance is very important.

I will admit that in this book I do focus more on the OUT polarity and for that reason there is a slight dis-balance in this book. The greater thrust of this book is about the mastery of Internal

> Manipulation, and how to use this technique to change your life and fight the oppressive dark forces that rule this world. The dis-balance created from the overemphasis on the OUT polarity provides the force / push / propellant needed to showcase a new way to act upon (and beat) the great Archon, and the great sum of humanity that are its unwitting pawns. It also provides the energy required to be able to present a true and complete Alchemical treatise.

The VOID polarity then, is incredibly powerful because it shows us how to navigate through this world in a way that permits us to give up as little energy as possible to it. It does this by allowing the Alchemist to contain his energetic makeup. When an Alchemist has mastered this polarity, he or she becomes 'A Babe in an Egg', silent and untouched by the world around them.

Because of the great power of this polarity, I will provide two techniques that I find very powerful in learning to master this energetic position. With these two techniques you should be able to get a good understanding of what it means to develop Energetic Containment and how to attain true silence yourself.

Exercise 1: First Level of Energetic Containment

With this first method, you will be using a similar technique to the one that I provided for the mastery of the IN polarity, this technique though is part of the VOID polarity:

- Try to find a quiet room where you can take a very comfortable sitting position, and where you will not be disturbed for at least 15 minutes to half an hour.
- If you will remember, in the last chapter I had you try to use the power of your mind to pull an object into yourself. This technique is similar, except in this technique you will not be trying to pull in an object or even foreign energy that is bothering you. Instead you will be trying to pull the greater some of your personal energetic makeup back into yourself.

You might find that this pulling IN of energy is somehow not appropriate in the mastery of the VOID polarity, being that instead of trying to find complete quietude you're actually pulling IN energy. But what is going on here is that you will be drawing in the energy that you have put out already, and when you do this you will be Containing that Energy, thanks to the powerful pull that you have hopefully developed using the 'Discovering and Using Your Psychic Energy Pumps' exercise that I mentioned in the last chapter. You are essentially using an energy pump to pull your spent energy back into yourself and you will also be using this pump to help you maintain/contain that energy so that it doesn't escape from you again.

- Once you have seated yourself in a quiet place, I want you to use that pulling force (or pump) to pull in all of the energy that you feel you are currently putting out into the atmosphere around you.

In this case you are not trying, and therefore not imagining, that you are pulling in energy from the things around you, but are now in fact just trying to pull in the energy that you have already put out in the form of strong emotion, reflexive reaction, and intense thought.

Another way to imagine this (visualization is VERY important in energy work) is to imagine that you feel that you are pulling into yourself the feelers that you use to perceive the world. Imagine that you are this odd creature that projects from itself these small tentacles, sort of like a tentacled amoeba that uses these appendages to perceive the world around it. Imagine then that it is these tentacles that you are pulling into yourself using that powerful Pull from the energy pump that you have developed.

You see, the act of perception, the active interaction with the world around you, is an energetic act. In order to perceive the world (and act within it), you need to project energy from yourself; the more energy that you can project out of yourself, the more powerfully that you can perceive or affect this exterior world Out There. By pulling in this energy that you quite naturally push out when you interact with the world in your everyday life, you are withdrawing yourself from this world and greatly reducing how much this world can affect you.

- As you pull your energy into yourself imagine that you pull in every single energetic tentacle, so that in a quite symmetrical way you pull in all of the energy from all around you until these energy tentacles come right to the very edge of your body, or to the very edge of what you consider to be yourself.

- Once you get to this point, what you need to do is contain and solidify that borderline between yourself and the outside world. In essence what you are doing, after you have pulled in all of your external energy, is to create the type of force field, a hard edge, around yourself that then contains your energetic essence.

- If you were to look at yourself from afar, and you could see the energy around you as you did so, you might notice that you have in some ways become like that babe in an egg, a being that knows true silence and detachment.

- Try to solidify the edges of this containment field and pull back any energy within this containment field that you feel is about to be projected out.

  You will note that any time that you have an emotional reaction, any time that you are forced to act impulsively either because you have been suddenly frightened or because you have had a reactive, reflexive, reaction to something, you will feel like some energy is being propelled from within you towards the outside world.

I often have people note how much tension they have in their body and how this tension shifts in position and intensity throughout the day. I then point out that any tension that they feel is an accumulation of energy and a point where they are potentially projecting energy into the environment.

In order for you to have an emotion, or even a strong feeling of any kind, you either need to generate this energy within yourself or you need to let in foreign energy from outside yourself that drives you to act in this way. Emotion, like physical action, is the result of energy accumulation and release.

No energy, no action. This energy which might be felt as a slight or very pronounced tension in the body, is pumped by the body musculature out of the body, either as a flash of intense emotion or as a simmering ebb of emotion or feeling.

By pulling your energy into yourself and by containing it within this force field that you have created, you attain the First Level of Energetic Containment.

What this means is that this level of Energetic Containment allows you to have great control over your emotions. This is indeed the way towards emotional control, something which is greatly prized but is seldom achieved.

I suggest that once you have developed mastery over this particular technique, that you take the time to go outside and interact people while you try to maintain this type of Energetic Control. If you have become good at this technique, you will note that you will be able to instantly sense a detachment within yourself. You will no longer be swayed by the emotions and the Intent of others, you will no longer experience exaggerated emotional outbursts, as your mind and the world around you presses one button or the other in order to try and get some kind of reaction from you; the more of a reaction that the world gets from you, the more distilled energy that you give to it.

And surprisingly, you might realize that once you have mastered this type of Energetic Containment, a great deal of happiness will flood over you. Again, I implore you not to lose yourself too much in the indulgences of these happy feelings and try to contain these Energetic Flares, but it is interesting to note that this first level of Energetic Containment can create a great deal of happiness while trying to create nothing at all.

> **Perfect joy is to be without joy.**
> CHUANG TZU,
> TRANSLATED BY THOMAS MERTON

You will note that the technique that I mention above can stop all emotional and impulsive Energetic Flares once it is mastered, but that it does not stop the mind from chattering. The reason for this is that Energetic Containment is maintained outside of the thinking mind. The barrier to the energy coming in and to the energy spilling out, is held in check like by a type of egg shaped force field around the body, so that the mind then is free to think as much as it wants.

This has its advantages, in that it allows the mind to function very well without the interruptions and the manipulations that can be so distracting when someone is trying to think logically and critically. Indeed, one could say that this First Level of Energetic Containment is perfect for the logical mind and critical thinking under trying circumstances.

But this first level of Energetic Containment still leaves that mind uncontained. This means that there is Energetic Containment over the body but the mind is left free to think what it wants. In order to contain the mind, the mind must be stopped, and in order to stop the mind all thoughts must be stopped. **The Second Level of Energetic Containment is achieved when one is able to master the ability to stop the thinking process.**

There are a number of different techniques that have been used throughout history and geographic regions. I have already mentioned the one technique of looking at a dot on the wall, or sometimes just looking at a bare wall. There are other techniques like closing your eyes and looking at the darkness behind your eyelids.

The problem with all these techniques though, is the fact that they take time; often they take years to master and require a great deal of attentive effort, which can be a difficult thing to manage if you are not dedicating yourself to this task on a full-time basis.

I therefore recommend employing a different technique, one that can help to completely stop internal conscious thought and that can also help one to move 'within' inner space.

This technique involves the disruption of a particular routine that has quite literally shaped the modern conscious human mind.

This routine is the sleep cycle; the sleep routine.

For the most part, humans sleep in a cycle that involves one very large wakeful time and another long sleep time. On average most humans sleep for about eight hours a day in one long sleep stretch and then are awake for the rest of the day.

This type of sleep cycle is really just a deeply rooted routine[1]. There is a great deal of evidence to show

---

[1] For further information on past sleep cycles and their effect on human culture, I would recommend the book *At Days Close: Night In Times Past* by A. Roger Ekirch.

that humanity has gone through a number of different sleep cycles in the past, and that this current sleep cycle is very much the result of what the rational mind believes the ideal sleep cycle should be. To the rational mind, sleep is a waste of time, and the best way to control this waste is to try and get it out of the way in one solid block, while at the same time try to reduce this sleep block as much as possible. As a result, we have our long stretch of sleep that people are always trying to shorten, and of course coffee has become an indispensable vice.

Exercise 2: Second Level of Energetic Containment

- In order to stop the mind, in order to stop the chatter, and that constant role of images and ideas that seem to endlessly scroll across the screen of the mind, I recommend doing something that might seem highly 'productive' to the rational mind; and that is to reduce the time that you spend sleeping.

    Now I don't want you to get carried away, and I don't mean for you to greatly reduce how much sleep you are getting. What I am actually suggesting is that you take a little tiny bit out of that long stretch of sleep that you go through every night, and use this time and this accumulated 'sleep energy' to help you stop your chattering mind for a while.

From a rational point of view; that is from a perceptive point where the world is an object filled place and you are just another object within it, one could say that lack of sleep increases the production of sleep hormones like melatonin and adenosine. By using these naturally produced 'mental propellants', these sleepy feeling hormones, we can stop the endless chatter of the mind.

From an Alchemical point of view, I would not use the term hormone because indeed one could say that sleep inducing hormones are a physical manifestation of an energetic accumulation. From an Energetic Cognitive Position, you could say that **you are creating a type of dis-balance that increases a certain type of energetic essence. Through the accumulation and transmutation of this energetic essence, you can use this amassed power to induce no-thought, and therefore open a doorway into new dimensions.**

- In order to do this, try and find out how much sleep you get a night. If for example you sleep about eight hours every night, I want you to try and reduce your sleep time to seven hours and forty-five minutes a night. That is, whatever amount of time you sleep, I want to try and reduce that amount by fifteen minutes.

> *Please talk to a physician before you do anything that you think might endanger your health. I am not a medical expert and whatever suggestions I make are for informational purposes only. I cannot take responsibility for your actions; I therefore suggest that you take all precautions before you engage in anything that you think might endanger your health. Also if you drive or usually work with big and dangerous equipment, this is not an exercise that you should try.*

- In order to create this energetic dis-balance, you need to reduce the amount of time that you sleep per night. This energetic accumulation (or the objective accumulation of the hormone melatonin if you wish to see things from an objective perspective) even for one or two days, can greatly increase the amount of energy that you have at your disposal. This will of course make you sleepy at times, especially just before you go to bed, or when you first wake up in the morning (meaning that it's going to get hard to pick yourself up out of that bed). But a discomfort like this is the price one pays for energy accumulation using dis-balance.

Now, what most people do when they start to get a bit sleepy is that they take a nap, or they try to drink a cup of coffee as quickly as possible. This sleepy feeling is looked at with great contempt by the modern person because it means that the Cognitive Position which greatly favors rational thinking has becomes a bit unstable; in other words, it's hard to think clearly.

What I would have you do though, instead of taking that nap or ingesting some kind of stimulant, is to make sure that you take some time during your day to use up that energy that you have accumulated in a more constructive way.

- To do this I want you to find a quiet room again where you can sit down and relax, where you won't be disturbed for a good 15 minutes to half an hour. I don't recommend lying down because in this position it is really easy to fall asleep.

- In this quiet place, I want you to close your eyes, and find the most comfortable sitting position possible. Then just relax and let that drowsy feeling wash over you.

- Imagine that that drowsiness that you are feeling is like an energetic wave that rolls across your body. As this energetic wave rolls across your body it will naturally relax your body and begin the process of shutting down the body for sleep. Eventually you will be feeling a bit cool as your blood pressure goes down, your limbs will begin to go limp, and even your senses will feel like they are shutting down, so that your focus of attention will naturally turn inwardly instead of being focused on the exterior world.

- You will also feel this energetic wave roll across your mind, seemingly rolling through the inside of your skull, turning off all the thoughts in your head. It is quite possible that you will begin to see images like swirling geometric patterns or even full-blown scenes that will make you believe that you are dreaming. This state that you are in is referred to as the hypnogogic state, and you can think of it as a Cognitive Position in between wakefulness and sleep.

- What I want you to do though, which can be a bit difficult depending on how sleepy you are, is to NOT focus your attention on these images, feeling and sensations, but instead to focus your attention on the flow of this sleepy energy as it deliciously moves throughout your body and mind.

In other words, your main goal here is to focus on the sleepy energy, and move that wonderfully relaxing energy throughout the body, particularly when it feels like its swirling inside your skull. What you don't want to do is to fall asleep and start dreaming.

- You will note that if you do this exercise when you become sleepy, that after fifteen minutes to half an hour later, this sleepy feeling will be greatly reduced. From an energetic perspective, you could say that you are using up this sleepy energy that you have accumulated, by distributing it through your body and brain. This sleepy energy will relax your body to the point where you will quite literally go limp, and it will stop all conscious thought within your mind if you purposefully move this sleepy feeling energy into your brain. You will essentially be stopping all conscious thought for the time that you can keep this sleepy energy flowing through your brain.

- Once you have attained this sleepy no-thought state, try to look around as it were. See if you can perceive anything while not thinking at all. Play with these sensations and the perceptions that you encounter. For example, your senses may begin to combine, so that you may see/feel that you are now in a room without walls, experiencing odd bodily sensations. You may remember odd events that never happened in 'real' conscious life. You may experience alterations that will jumble cause and effect, so that the things that you experience might seem crazy, random, and purposeless. As a result you may begin to believe that this new Cognitive Position is just chaotic madness, but this is not the case; what is actually happening is that your mind is currently not able to deal with the speed and the spaciousness of the internal sense data that it is now perceiving. In time your mind will adjust and learn, and your intellect will grow accordingly.

At this point, you have attained The Second Level of Energetic Containment...something that some practitioners in the past have devoted a lifetime of effort to achieve.

I provide this exercise for Second Level Energetic Containment for your own personal development efforts. YOU WILL NOT need to master it in order to become adept at the techniques that will ultimately become the core of this book's intent; which is to fight against the Great Archon.

In this book our ultimate end is to master the Alchemical Triad so that we can increase personal Will Force/Intent and fight against the oppression of/from the world; both from other humans and from the predatory non-organic Alien Force that now has a controlling interest over mankind. In order to do that, First Level Energetic Containment is most important because is it this ability that will allow you to stop the taxing nature of constant Energetic Flares and energy drainage.

I implore you then to practice First Level Containment on a regular basis as often as you can; first in private as a meditative exercise, and eventually in public as a way to control all emotions and contain energy.

Through this powerful technique you will quickly feel a detachment from this hectic world, which will be very pleasant, and you will as a result begin to note just how much energy you are giving up to silly things that at the end of the day really don't matter. This drain ages us; it makes us tired and as a result, complacent. It takes away our edge and turns our lives into safe routine and grey drudgery. The more we lose, the older and weaker we become until one day we wake up and find that we are so old that we just don't want to get out of bed anymore.

But now you have a way to fight this drain, a way to fight this deliberately created cage designed to drain all your power. In Chapter 9 I will expand on the techniques presented here and I will show you how to use them in real life situations.

But before we do that, we need to learn about the most important polarity, in relation to what this book is trying to achieve. We first need to learn about the OUT polarity!

CHAPTER 6
Going OUT

One man's 'magic' is another man's engineering. 'Supernatural' is a null word.
ROBERT A. HEINLEIN

If we contemplate what we have discussed so far, in the simplest of terms we could say that we have learned how to suck energy into ourselves, and how to seal that energy within so that the world does not rob us of our gains.

Suck, contain, suck, contain...

These techniques represent two thirds of the energetic makeup of a human being and as such are very powerful. If you could master these two polarities you could advance beyond this world if you like, or if you wish to remain here, you could certainly live a long physical existence full of relative peace and vigor.

Unfortunately, we share this Earth with other human beings like ourselves and we also need to contend with a megalithic Alien Force that can crush us with its mighty Intent. What this means fundamentally is that we need claws.

We need a way to move freely in this world, as fully individual beings that have the possibility of accomplishing anything that we might desire.

The ability to break our cage so that we can have the freedom to be what we want, to be and do what we want, is what this book is really all about. And the one polarity that concerns itself more than any other with this ability is the OUT polarity!

This chapter gives you the basic principles of how to begin to fight against a world that seems to be designed to make us fearful, worried, tired, and miserable. **By learning to master the OUT polarity, we learn how to protect energy OUTSIDE of ourselves; OUT into that Dark Sea that surrounds us all, and in this way project our Will, and then our Intent, into that world.**

In order to understand why it is critical to master the OUT polarity, we could simplify matters; which is never truly a good thing in the long run, but it does help to clarify things when we are first learning something new. Simply then we could say that there are two basic types of Alchemists in the world:

- The first type of Alchemists is perhaps the one that is most commonly thought of when you think of the ideal of the lone mystic. This type of Alchemists is usually interested in detaching him or herself from the world. He or she is interested in the mastery of the VOID polarity which he first uses to break free from all the people and limiting Intent around him, and then uses this polarity to break away from the world by escaping into the unknown using his or her Astral Body **(And this is generally the ONLY time that this type of Alchemist uses the OUT polarity).**

This type of Alchemists is the iconic hermit of the mountains as it were, that tries to find solitude and distance where he or she is free to store as much energy as possible, and to concentrate all of his or her efforts into moving away from this Earthly vibrational position in order to engage in forays into the infinitude that awaits us, Out There.

Such an Alchemist is an incredibly intrepid individual who tackles the great unknown head on. Unfortunately, such detachment is not possible for the average person, and the life of such an Alchemist is most likely not possible for most of the readers of this book.

- The second type of Alchemist is the type of Alchemist that is very much of an old school variety. I say this because it was this type of Alchemist that first discovered how to manipulate energy so effectively by borrowing (a nicer word than stealing) the techniques employed by non-organic lifeforms. [If you are interested in finding out more about these ancient Alchemists, then I suggest you watch this YouTube video: https://youtu.be/HJpkb4goD6I. The video starts out discussing the modern Vampire culture but does in the end give a good, concise history of the first Alchemist and those non-organic beings that they owe everything to.]

These ancient Alchemists were predatory beings, just like the creatures they once worshipped. They were (and are) very much interested in this objective world that all humans share, and were/are deeply interested in acquiring and using the power that they were able to squeeze out of it. These Alchemists were somber, grim, dark, and highly determined sorcerers that were completely focused on the manipulation of their external reality through internal techniques like Internal Manipulation.

Alchemists that resemble those ancient 'Lofty Ones' are interested in ingesting and storing as much energy as possible, which they take from the world around them with no consideration for others. They then use this energy to shape the world into whatever they desire using very powerful OUT polarity techniques.

This type of Alchemist is interested in detachment only to the point that it allows him or her to store far greater amounts of energy, and they are deeply interested in mastering the ability to suck in as much energy as possible from his or her surroundings, because more energy means more potential to push OUT and therefore greater power.

As in all things within the realm of Alchemy, extremes are never a good thing and it is always best that we find balance. Balance here can be found by looking at and contemplating these two extremes, and using the strengths from both to create something that can work in your life.

Fundamentally though, true balance can only be achieved by making sure that we treat each polarity with equal regard, and engage ourselves in trying to master all three.

While it is not good to take from others without their consent and to manipulate only for completely egoistic ends, we must also realize that we live in a tough world that cannot be ignored. Stated plainly: **just because you ignore the tiger, that does not mean that the tiger will ignore you!**

In this world, to survive and thrive, we need to be a little bit mystic and a little bit sorcerer too!

And so we find ourselves the gates of the final polarity, the OUT Tri-polarity:

Within the realm of this OUT polarity we uncover our instrument for action, our magic wand; the pointy end of that which I refer to as Internal Manipulation. Through the mastery of this polarity we can change our world and create a life that best suits our personal ideals. The OUT polarity helps to move energy within the body (which I refer to as Will Power) and it allows us to project energy from it as well (which I refer to as Intent).

Will is a dynamic force that is little understood when we think of it in purely rational terms, but that can be clearly understood if we think of things from an energetic perspective. From this energetic perspective, we realize that Will is an actual force, a force that we have to fastidiously work to accumulate and direct. Will therefore, is that stored energy within the Alchemist that now has the potential to become something else.

And thanks to this stored POTENTIAL, we have the ability to project energy through the OUT polarity. This OUT energy is first understood as Will Power when it is used to change our own being. It then has the further POTENTIAL of becoming Intent when our Will Power is strong enough to create a current outside of ourselves in the Dark Sea. These self-created currents can take us anywhere we want to go, and can change the people and the world around us in accordance with our desires.

When we look at the Dark Sea with our regular eyes, we see a world full of objects. But if you are, I hope, now willing to contemplate the possibility that the world is actually a sea of energy, then you must accept the possibility that all these objects that we all take for granted might just be a type of illusion; symbols that hide greater mysteries. This illusion is caused by something that I have referred to as a Cognitive Position or Cognitive Perspective.

Furthermore, in this book I present the idea that this Cognitive Perspective is an 'imposed' perceptive stance that is the consequence of a foreign Intent of titanic proportions, and that this very powerful Intent is being projected by a colossal non-organic life form that is solely interested in consuming humanities energetic essence.

By pushing OUT energy ourselves, and creating new currents in the Dark Sea, we are able to fight against this dark force Out There. We fight this Alien Intent by creating our own Intent, so that we can create a new conscious life in the pursuit of our true selves through the manifestation/transmutation of our personal values and ideals.

Pushing energy OUT allows us to create/manifest/transmute/bring-about the things that we desire by either re-modulating the vibrational frequency of parts of the Dark Sea, or by adjusting our own movement through the Dark Sea so that we run smack into that thing or situation that we desire.

The OUT polarity is interested in the seemingly magical reshaping of our world. To become a master of the OUT polarity is to become 'The Magician'.

There is a great deal of material out there on how to perform many different types of spells, how to do ceremonial magic, create sigils, and how to manifest what you want using various energetic practices like the Law of Attraction. There are good systems out there that try to teach you how to get what you want, and how to manifest what you desire.

What very few of these informational sources mention though is how it is that you go about getting better at, getting what you want. They will usually provide some decent techniques that you can employ in order to get what you desire, like performing some powerful magical act for example, but they seldom discussed why it is that some people seem to have very good results while other people hardly ever get any good results at all.

Those that provide good technique, will often times discuss how these techniques can be improved and how the mastery of certain techniques in the right order and with the right amount of potency can increase your success. But generally speaking there seems to always be this hit and miss that is seldom discussed in a satisfactory way.

Alchemists have a very simple answer for this hit and miss success rate, which as you might suspect comes down to one basic thing; energy.

Quite simply: the more energy that you have, the more that you can create/manifest/transmute into existence. The more Will Force (Potential) that you have to push OUT upon the world, the more that you can do.

And as I have said before, no one polarity is more important than any of the others. Each one contributes to the others, so it is the case that in order become more successful at transmutation/manifestation, you need to become better at acquiring and sustaining power. In order to gain this power you need to be able to pull (IN) more of it in from the environment around you, and you need to be able to seal it (VOID) within yourself until the time that you need to use it.

In the last two chapters we discussed how to gain this power and also how to maintain it. In this chapter we learn how to use it, how to project it effectively. As we continue though, do remember what I said about Potential, about the need to be able to have more in order to be able to do more. This means that it is very important that you know how to draw energy from the world and how to sustain this energy so that it is not wasted on silly indulgences and is instead used for good purpose.

To begin, we need to first know what projecting energy feels like, an incredibly crucial aspect of manifestation/transmutation that is seldom discussed.

In order to do this, think back to the exercise where I had to pull an object like a cup from on top of a table. You would rightly suppose that trying to push that object away from you is quite essentially the act of projecting energy OUT.

I want you therefore to repeat that exercise but this time I want you to try and push that cup away from you. Don't push too hard, moving or not moving the object is not what is important, what is important is that you get a feel for what pushing energy OUT feels like.

The projection of energy requires a great deal of effort and there is most likely going to be some kind of strain on your body, and this stress, or rigidity of body, is easily identifiable to someone paying attention to what you are doing. For this reason, I find such stressful projection of energy is an all right thing to engage in when you are alone at home perhaps and wish to try and manifest something.

I feel though that this book is much more about the act of engaging life on a face-to-face level. What I mean by this is that I want to provide a technique that you can use anytime and anywhere, and that no one, unless they are paying a great deal of close attention to you, will be able to know that you are 'doing' anything at all.

As such, it is important to note that the most important aspect of using our personal Intent to free ourselves from the Intent of the world at large, is to let go as much as possible of direct physical action. The first place to begin in letting go of this physical action is to use a type of Internal Action that is not externally perceptible. I refer to this Internal Action as **Internal Manipulation**.

Why is there such a need for covert internal action?

The reason is that we, like our animal brothers, have many territorial instincts. And even though we consider ourselves to be quite civilized, it is obvious (if you spent any time around people) that we still engage in many territorial battles every day.

Body language is something that is scrutinized intently by all the people around us, whether they realize what they are doing instinctually or not. People use these body language indicators to judge what others are intending and therefore what they should do to defend against those intentions.

In order to see this territorial posturing in action, all you need to do is to go into any crowded place; my personal choice would be the grocery store. In the grocery store, where with a cart or a basket in hand, people are quite primitively foraging for food, you can see just how territorial we still are and how even the smallest physical actions can have consequences.

You will note that if you get excited about some particular item in the store for example, others around you will read such cues and will turn to see what you are looking at; some may even rush in front of you to try and get to this product before you by blocking your way. You will even note that some very aware and astute shoppers will quite consciously keep a close eye on where others look or gravitate towards because this might tell them where there might be a sale, or a special product that they might have missed.

You may also note that walking down an aisle, becomes more and more difficult as the amount of people in the store increases. From a logical perspective this would seem to have an obvious reason; the more people, the less room, and the more competition for the products in the store. Many though forget to add the full power of psychology into this calculation and underestimate the increased emotional charge that such an increased population can generate. This emotional charge will have people taking up more room in the isles and will cause them to get in your way more often as they try to assert their dominance. This creates a great deal of psychic energy that can easily be converted into physical outburst of sometimes violent proportions.

Large crowds can be a dangerous thing. If enough individual minds focus in one direction, this strong current generated by them will drag the rest of the group in that direction as well. This means that if you go against the mob you will be punished, and if you are caught up in desperate mob intent, then don't be surprised if you too begin to act in the most primitive and unconscious way possible. In order to see the truth of this, all you have to do is try to participate in a large Black Friday sale.

Such territorial body language and actions are part of our daily lives as human beings, vestiges some might say of our primate ancestors, as they fought for survival and dominance. As such, the act of pushing energy OUT can be quite a complicated thing when surrounded by a large crowd because this can make you stand out as a potential weirdo or trouble maker, and you might therefore incur the wrath of the mob.

This is definitely what we don't want. And for that reason, in this book I will be showing how the project energy in a most natural way, a way that will not have you becoming rigid with effort as you stare intently, which can make you stand out like a sore thumb and can have negative social connotations.

In order to understand this most natural way of projecting energy to get what you want, we need to understand the individual components that make it possible. This understanding is necessary because it will allow you to really refine the process and take it from an unconscious impulse into a conscious act that you can control, refine, and make much stronger.

The three basic aspects that make up this natural Will Force action are:

1. The act of focusing your attention
2. The act of breathing OUT
3. Emotion

Focused Attention

Focused attention is the most powerful and natural energy funnel that we have. We create our world through our attention, and if you remember back to Chapter 2, you will remember that the act of paying attention also collapses potential probabilities; which further helps to solidify the world for us. The act of paying attention propels energy from inside an aware being: **The act of perception is thc act of creation!**

Here is where 'Potential' comes back into the picture. The more energy that we have, that is the more energy that we can draw from the world around us and the more energy that we can sustain within ourselves, the more powerful that our attention becomes.

You could ask yourself why it is that some people seem smarter or perhaps even more dedicated, more capable, more successful, and better at mental work. Interestingly, you could also ask yourself why it is that some people seem to be so darn unsuccessful and unlucky. Even when everything seems to be in their favor at first, they seem to be able to reverse this good fortune very quickly and step right into the worst luck possible over and over again.

The answer to this is their ability to pay more attention; their ability to be able to narrow the focus of their attention to only what they want (or don't want) for extended periods of time. When they can control the focus of this powerful attention on good things, they seem to be unstoppable luck machines, but when they can only focus on the worst thing possible, they seem to walk with a dark cloud above their heads.

This ability to focus intently can be the result of a natural talent that they were born with, or it can be the result of them being able to accumulate and sustain more energy than others. Whatever they pay attention to; they will most likely move towards and create in their lives because the power of their attention is more powerful than the average persons.

Some people wonder why it is that they seem to try all of the methods and techniques expounded by mind power gurus, but they are seldom able to get the results that they would like. These gurus sometimes point out that attention and the ability to focus, or visualize in some way, is very important. If they are good teachers, they might even suggest certain exercises in order to try and help develop this attention. What is never mentioned, at least in the books that I have read on the subject, is the fact that this **attention can indeed be developed to some degree through exercises, but the true measure of a person's ability to pay attention and to maintain that attention for sustained periods of time, has everything to do with how much energy they have.**

In this book I have shown you how to acquire that energy, and conserve it. Now it is time to use that energy in order to focus and develop your attention, so that you can get what you want in a way that will be good for you and for all those around you as well. And in a way that will allow you to exercise your Will Power, your Intent, without anyone ever suspecting that you are a practitioner of Internal Manipulation.

To master the first component of natural Will Force projection, I want to find a nice quiet place, where you can take a comfortable position and spend about 15 minutes to half an hour performing the following:

Exercise: Visualization Through Focused Attention

- Start by simply paying attention to something. Focus your attention on that one thing for as long as possible.

   I don't want you to focus your attention on any one object that might be around you now. What I want to do is to try and visualize something in your mind, and then try and keep your focused attention on that visualization for as long as possible.

   When we speak of visualization, what we most often think about is a mental picture. The thing is though that visualization involves far more than just a picture in your head, even though the ability to visualize a vivid mental image like this is indeed very important.

   There are then a myriad of different types of visualizations possible, but the basic three are directly related to how we perceive using our physical senses. These big three are as follows:

- visual image; this means a clear and vivid picture in your mind's eye.
- an auditory sensation; that is the ability to vividly imagine a sound, the ability to visualize sound in your mind.
- A kinesthetic sensation; the ability to visualize a feeling, either external to ourselves or internal.

- Let us begin then by exercising the ability to visualize a VISUAL image. I know that there are some people out there that say that they cannot visualize a visual image at all, and that some of these people tend to believe that because of this inability, they are greatly hampered when it comes to these kinds of energetic or magical practices.

The thing is though, that it is indeed quite rare to not be able to do these kinds of Visual visualization, whether you believe it or not, and unless you have had some kind of brain trauma, we can all visualize a visual image to a greater or lesser degree. Any time that you have a memory of something, it is most likely that you are remembering a visual memory. For example, if I ask you to remember what you did 10 minutes ago, it is quite likely the that you will have a visual image of what you were doing, like perhaps seeing yourself turning on your computer.

- If you are having trouble visualizing a visual image, try instead to remember something from your past.

  For this exercise for example, I want you to 'close your eyes' and visualize within your mind's eye the image of an apple. If you think that you are having trouble or that you can't visualize such an image, I want to find a picture of an apple on your computer or wherever else you might be able to get one and then try to remember that image.

- Now here's the important part, I don't want you to try and stress in any way while you are doing this. That is I don't want you to try and work really hard at seeing the apple, or at seeing this apple as vividly real as possible. What I want to do is just to keep your attention focused on an apple, on the image of what this apple might be or can be (or once was if you are remembering an image).

  What you will find when you do this, is that this apple might be quite fragmented inside your mind's eye. This apple will probably not be perfect, it will most likely not be shaped property, it might move around on you and change shape, the color might not be distinct, and you might find it difficult to keep your attention on this apple, meaning that you might begin to think of other things.

What I want you to do though is to keep bringing your mind, the focus of your attention, back to this somewhat abstract and jagged visualization of this particular apple. The trick here is to maintain your attention focused on this apple in a relaxed way for as long as possible.

- As you do so, you might begin to notice that this apple will become far more concrete inside your mind's eye. This visual visualization will begin to take on better shape or form, the color will become more vibrant and more seemingly real to you, and a part of you might actually begin to believe that this apple is there in the darkness inside your mind.

What is happening here is that your attention is quite naturally making this apple more and more real. It does this by quite naturally pumping energy into this visual visualization; turning it from a somewhat convoluted initial image, to a far more concrete and seemingly real one. It is indeed the case that the more attention that you can project onto this visualization, the more real that this apple will become.

It is like this with all things, the more energy that things gain energetically, the more real and the more concrete that they become. As a self-aware energy bundle, you are able to direct the direction and focus of your attention to anything you want. The more attention that you give a thing, the more energy that you can pump into/onto that thing, which changes that things Energetic Mass and Vibrational frequency.

What this means is that you can turn one thing into another thing just through the focus of your attention, which is truly the Alchemical process, and it is quite simply the case then that we are all Alchemists whether we realize it or not!

And so, I want you to just focus your attention on this 'visual' visualization of an apple in the most focused way that you can for as long as you can, and watch what happens. By doing this you will quickly discover the creative power that is within you, as this particular apple becomes more and more real in your mind.

- When you are satisfied that you have a pretty decent visual visualization of an apple in your mind's eye, I want you to open your eyes and looked about the room you are in. If your visual visualization was not perfect, then don't worry because such visualizations will get better and better over time, as you become better at focusing your attention and allowing your energy to naturally flow into the things that you are paying attention to.

But now, with your eyes open, completely aware of the room around you, I want you to once again try to see this visual visualization of an apple. The thing is though that now I want you to see this visualization floating before you in this room with your eyes open!

Again do not try to force the image into existence, just keep your focus of attention on a particular spot in the room where you think this apple might be floating, and then let the focus of your attention pump energy into this visualization so that it becomes more and more real the more that you focus upon it.

In time, you should see this apple becoming more and more real, taking on form, perhaps developing better color, and even developing a type of three-dimensional presence within the space of the room. It is quite likely that this apple might go from being quite vividly there, to fading out and becoming not as real, only to become a little more real yet again. What is happening here is that such fluctuations indicate the fluctuations of your attention. As your attention wanes and deviates your apple's structure will also fluctuate, and in this way you will discover the limits of your attention and you will also be able to use these fluctuations as a type of biofeedback in order to better develop your attention over time.

I want you to try and do this exercise for about 15 minutes. This is a pretty long time to focus your attention on one thing if you have not done anything like this before, so do take it easy at first. If you want, you don't have to go for a full 15 minutes the first time, you could try for 5 minutes and work your way to a full 15 minutes. I want you to get to the point though where you can keep your attention focused on your visualization for a full fifteen minutes.

I think you will be incredibly surprised at how vivid these visualizations will become without much effort on your part at all.

- Next, I want to you repeat the same exercise above but this time try to visualize a feeling. First it is good to note that there are two general types of feelings and these can be said to be:
    - internal: a feeling that you have inside like an emotion, or the certainty of a belief.
    - external: a feeling that you have that you could say comes from outside your body, like feeling cold or feeling the rough surface of a wall.

- First pick an external feeling like for example the feeling of a nice breeze hitting your face, and then I want you to focus your attention on this feeling for a good 15 minutes until the power of your attention makes this 'feeling' visualization as vividly real as possible. Do remember not to push it though, just focus your attention and relax your body.

  Next I want you to do the same exercise but with an internal feeling. You could for example imagine what it might feel like to have just won the lottery. Focus your attention on this abstract concept; what it would be like to win the lottery, what emotions and internal sensations you might feel if you won that great prize.

  Again you will notice that as you focus your attention on it, and let your attention naturally develop the reality of this feeling, you will begin to experience what this feeling must be like. Keep a close eye on the fluctuation in your feelings, as these will clearly show you the limits of your attention. Try to do this exercise for 15 minutes as well.

- Finally I want to work on an auditory visualization. To do this I would suggest that you try to imagine (visualize), what it might be like to hear a musical instrument. You could for example imagine what it might be like to hear a beautiful piano playing in the background.

Again I don't want you to stress in trying to make this auditory visualization real, what I want to do is to focus your attention on the possibility of this visualization and let the power of your attention developed this 'auditory' visualization naturally. In time, if your focus of attention is strong enough, you will begin to hear this piano playing and you might even be surprised at how real this auditory visualization becomes.

After you have done this for 15 minutes, I want you to say a certain word or phrase out loud. You could for example say, "I am happy". Then focus your attention on the memory of the sound of this phrase. I want you to focus your attention on remembering hearing that phrase, "I am happy". See if you can focus your attention on the memory of that phrase for 15 minutes. See if you can eventually clearly hear yourself saying that phrase in your mind.

Try to do these exercises at least two times a week for a month if you can. You might find that these visualizations become quite fun, especially after you realize that there is no effort involved aside from the development of your attention. And that instead of visualizing boring things like apples, you can visualize anything that seems pleasing to you.

These exercises will teach you about the OUT Tri-polarity and what it is like to push OUT energy in the most natural way possible.

As you do these exercises, you might notice that your power of attention will begin to wane over time. This is so because your attention, like everything else in our human existence is energy based. Once you expend a certain amount of energy, you need to replenish that energy in order to carry on.

This is something that is seldom mentioned by mind power gurus and it is unfortunate because not knowing this can have you scrambling to find out why you just can't seem to maintain that focus of attention on what you want throughout the day; like some of these gurus might advocate. No one can maintain a constant OUT projection of energy forever, just like we all can't breathe OUT forever; there is a point when we are all forced to breathe IN.

Breathing OUT

In order to fix this lack of attention energy problem we can do two things;

a. we can shift back to the IN polarity so that we may absorb more energy (which we will discuss in the next chapter)
b. or we can breathe OUT as we visualize; which will help to channel whatever energy we have left in the direction of our attention and allow the natural flow of breathing to help revitalize our attention.

Breathing OUT is a very powerful and natural way to augment the power that we are using to perform any task.

To do this I want you to first focus your attention on whatever it is that you want to visualize, like in the above exercise, and then once you have that visualization in focus, I want you to try and breathe out as slowly and naturally as possible.

Think of your lungs as being a large glass of water, when you fill a glass of water, that is when you breathe IN, you fill this glass from the bottom to the top. And when you wish to empty this glass, that is when you breathe OUT, you empty this glass from the top to the bottom. When you breathe OUT therefore,

I want you to feel that the air in your lungs is being expelled from the very top to the bottom of your lungs.

When you do need to breathe IN, I want you to make this inhalation as quick as and as natural as possible so that you are filling your lungs from the bottom to the top in a quick IN breath. Once this IN breath is finished, I want you to once again slowly breathe OUT and try to maintain that sharp and narrow focus of attention on the thing that you are visualizing.

You will note as you breathe OUT, the power of your attention becomes more and more pronounced the longer that you can breathe OUT; that is the vividness of your visualization will increase as your lungs empty more and more. This increase is due to the fact that at the end of the OUT breath, there is a greater concentration of force being expelled in a very narrow band of awareness, which is then being focused by your attention on the thing that you are visualizing.

The performance of this OUT breath can also be highly important when you are in a social situation and you find that you become somewhat emotional or tense in any way. Essentially what you do is that when you become emotional or tense in any one particular situation, you breathe OUT. This breathing OUT allows you to re-channel (re-direct) the energy that you are expending on this emotional indulgence into the focus of your Will, so that instead of wasting energy on an emotion that is not helping you, you are directing it instead towards getting what you want through Will Force/visualization.

Practice with this technique in order to discover what works best for you in whatever situations you might encounter. Breathing OUT, the body naturally projects energy into other parts of itself for extra strength, or into mental activities in order to increase focus and intensity. **By learning to use the OUT breath in a conscious way, we supercharge everything that we do.**

Emotion

The final element behind the powerful projection of Will Force is the ability to channel emotions. Emotional energy is perhaps the most powerful concentration of energy that we human beings have, and if we could learn to harness this energy properly, it could quite literally propel us to the moon.

The thing is though that having an intense emotion on command is quite a difficult thing that can take years to master. Thankfully there is a natural way to access the power of attention, breath, and emotions.

This natural way to access our inherent power available through the OUT Polarity is; desire.

But before we learn about the power of 'Desire as Action', we have to first learn about the Push and Pull of life and how to overcome all obstacles through the mastery of the 'Supreme Ultimate'.

CHAPTER 7
The Supreme Ultimate and Refining the IN Polarity

I have never grown out of the infantile belief that the universe was made for me to suck.
ALEISTER CROWLEY

Every human being is a collection of energy bound together by a conglutinating force. The conglutinating force is quite simply the force of life because it is the only thing that is holding each individual human being together. As this conglutinating force begins to wane over time, as a result of lost and used up energy, a person begins to loose energetic stability. This lack of energetic stability is experienced through the physical senses as aging, and all of the physical maladies that are part and parcel of the aging process.

This energy bundle that is held together by the conglutinating life force is given a basic form by a vibrational matrix referred to as the human mold. This human mold imposes a basic shape on the bundle of energy held together by the conglutinating force and endows this form with all of the knowledge and skills necessary for the individual's survival on this planet.

Human beings therefore are perfectly designed to not only survive but thrive in this world. They also have the potential to access all the skills and knowledge that they might ever need to survive. Moreover, as long as Energetic Containment is maintained, the conglutinating force that keeps a person alive will not wane so quickly, which means that every human being on this planet has the potential to live for a very long time; certainly far longer than modern life expectancy.

As long as we don't let our conscious mind override this natural knowing, that naturally maintains the energetic flow between the three polarities, we can quite easily and quite powerfully manipulate our reality in order to fulfill ourselves in the most efficient and natural way possible.

There are old stories that say that in the very distant past we humans were amazing magical beings. At that time our energy flowed naturally and our existence was far different than the life we have now. The feats of perception that humanity could perform at that time were legendary and if you look at some of the old manuscripts that speak of these ancient humans, you will note that they were referred to as 'legendary men' or as 'the great men of old'.

When such old manuscripts are of good quality and well translated, from whatever ancient language, they do make it clear that such legendary beings were perfect because of the fact that they lacked one very important trait; an individual mind. They lacked the ego as we understand the term, which means that they had no awareness of the 'I' self.

At that time humanity did not have a particular 'I' compartment within the self. There was no separation between the environment, other human beings, and the individual self.

In this modern time we see ourselves as separate from the world, individual beings looking out into an 'Out There'. In those days, those people did not see an Out There, they were the out there. They were one with the earth, the weather, nature, and the animals. Humanity knew where best to live in order to avoid any danger, it could talk with the flora and the fauna as naturally as we now talk with each other, and it could perform feats of physical and perceptual movement that are now considered fantasy.

But for all our power and ability, we lacked an 'I' self and therefore lived a quiet existence without desire or aspiration.

Some mystics say that this was a perfect existence and that we should all aspire to go back to it. Such individuals tend to focus a great deal of effort in perfecting the VOID Tri-polarity, and rejecting the other two. They feel that the individual 'I' is an aberration that must be destroyed, and in some ways they are not wrong because the 'I' self that we now have become, could indeed be called a type of aberration.

Others though, point out that a part of man must have yearned for something more; for complete self-awareness, for the knowledge of true individual awareness and individual fulfillment. This, they think is what beckoned that Alien presence that took over a part of human awareness and placed upon it a foreign mind, an Alien Installation.

This foreign installation gave humanity what it had beckoned; it gave it an 'I' self, individual self-awareness. This alien installation/Intent provided self-awareness but in doing this it

shattered humanity's connection to everything, and man the magical being was gone; man was quite literally expelled from paradise.

No longer was humanity one with all things. This link to nature and to the energetic reality of life was broken, and so he hid and ran in fear from the world.

From that day on, the individual man and woman developed, becoming the human race as we now understand it. This humanity, separated from true knowledge, now finds itself in a difficult position because it has become scared and considers itself flawed, ashamed of its own reflection, full of raging emotions, and unbeknownst to most; food for an otherworldly force.

Think of a time when humanity knew everything, a time when it understood everything, a time when it could do almost anything, and was part of everything. And now think of our current state, and how little we know, how superstitious we are, how divided, how emotionally unstable, and generally how scared we modern humans are.

This is why the sages admonish us to fight against this Alien Mind (which they unfortunately just refer to as the ego) so that we may return to our true power and our magical place in nature, at one with the totality of the Dark Sea.

Alchemists though see things in slightly different way. For an Alchemist the foreign mind is not an evil invader that must be vanquished per se, it is an ally, a natural aspect of the Dark Sea itself.

Humanity beckoned this change, a part of itself desired this evolution into greater 'self' fulfillment, and the Dark Sea provided for man in true energetic fashion; it provided humanity with a way to have this 'I' self that it longed to have, but it did it in the only energetically feasible way:

Within the energetic realm, nothing is free; if something is given, something else must be taken away. In order to get this 'I' self, humanity must give back with equal measure. What humanity gives back is energy; a special kind of distilled energy that only it can provide.

The Foreign Mind is here to feed itself, to take from us, but we get something from it as well, we get the knowledge of true self-awareness; we get an individual 'I' awareness.

It might seem like a pretty one sided deal right now, we must have been conned most would argue. The thing is though that we are mere fledglings at this 'me' thing and since a silent part of us remembers what we were and where we came from, we know deep down that something is missing, so we now long for something that was lost; that power that we left behind.

Alchemy though is about evolution, about change and purification into a higher state. An Alchemist does not seek to give up his or her individuality so that he or she might once again find paradise in self disillusion. **An Alchemist wants his cake and wants to eat it too!**

An Alchemist is a daring creature interested in wrestling individuality from its current trap. He wants to take this individuality with him into the fantastic outer cosmos Out There.

In other words, an Alchemist wants to find the balance between knowledge of the individual self and the instinctual egoless knowledge of the 'legendary man' of the past. In order to do this an Alchemist needs to accumulate energy and to use that acquired power to wrestle free from the Alien Intent that holds his or her newly acquired individual awareness hostage.

The Great Dark Sea, in its energetic perfection has provided a way for a daring person to steal that individuality; it has provided a way to have individuality without the need for the foreign Alien Mind. **The way to freedom is through the challenge of life!**

Almost every person on Earth is born and dies as a slave. People are born into this world and soon after become indoctrinated into a system designed to take as much energy as possible from them, until the day comes when they finally lose all their energy and die; an awareness bubble is created by the churning sea, moves a little within this sea, and is destroyed by that same pressure that will create another awareness bubble somewhere else.

Throughout this small journey from one point in the Dark Sea to another, almost every single thought that this self-aware energetic bubble will have, won't be its own. It will be an implant, an imposed thought created by a foreign power that gives with one hand and takes double with the other.

But if this awareness bubble, as it makes its way through its Life Cycle, can realize that most of its thoughts are not its own and that it is now in a trap; it can realize that is has a chance to have a chance. It can realize just how special and capable it can be, how infinitely mysterious this world really is, and most importantly how it can gain enough Potential to realize at least some of those amazing capabilities.

This life is our challenge, the place where the self-aware human bubble can perfect its energetic control. If it can perfect its ability to manipulate energy well enough, it has a chance to wrestle its individuality away from the Alien Trap and take this individuality on journeys beyond all current conceivable possibility.

But how do we begin to take part in this challenge?

Once we have even the vaguest notion that we are in a perceptual trap, we start by doing everything that we can to escape that trap. Escaping that trap means first and foremost that we must begin to gain as much energy as we can, and then use that energy to help perfect our Will Power. In the world of regular affairs this means that we use that power to shape our lives and the world around us in accordance to what we desire, that which will provide for us our greatest personal fulfillment.

To do this, I find it most helpful to introduce a set of techniques that would seem to be more appropriate within the realm of the martial arts than the realm of mind power or Alchemy.

As I mention before, certain religious and philosophical disciplines tended to favor one polarity above the others which creates dis-balance over time, but I did mention that there were some that were quite inclusive, indeed if taught properly, they could be said to be nearly complete Alchemical treaties in and of themselves.

One of these disciplines is 'Old School' Taoism. Taoism is a very ancient discipline that involves a great deal of energetic work and provides the foundation for Eastern Alchemy. Ancient Taoist Alchemist's had a very reliable and thorough understanding of the energetic properties of the world around us, and were able to develop many techniques to increase their vitality and their intellectual capabilities.

As part of these energetic techniques that they developed over hundreds of years, lay the foundation for what later would be referred to as the 'Supreme Ultimate'.

This Supreme Ultimate was essentially a way to combine energetic principles with certain physical movements in order to ease energetic flow and develop ways to use that energy in the objective world. In the beginning this Supreme Ultimate, which later would be called Tai Chi, was a relatively physically static technique where a practitioner performed small movements to move energy throughout their bodies for health, vitality, and eventually external manipulation of reality for combat and self-defence.

As Tai Chi evolved, more and more physical movements were added in order to help with the distribution of energy through the body. These physical movements became part of the combat and self-defense aspect of Tai Chi. Initially these moves could perfectly combine both internal and external energetic manipulation.

In modern times, Tai Chi is more moving meditation than anything else and few know the full extent of the internal aspects of this Supreme Ultimate martial style.

One of the most iconic aspects of Tai Chi is the Yin-Yang model. Most people are familiar with this concept and even more people are familiar with the iconography that describes it.

This Yin-Yang symbol represents two polarities within the Tri-polarity that makes up the complete system of Alchemy. These two polarities represent:

- the IN and OUT
- the push and pull
- the empty and full
- the absorbing the expelling
- the soft and the hard

As such, you could say that in order to learn to manipulate within this world properly, in accordance with Alchemical technique, you must learn a type of Tai Chi; an older form, one that is based more on the manipulation of energy and far less on the manipulation of your physical body or other physical bodies for that matter.

At its foundation, this technique of Internal Manipulation is very simple because all energetic movement is fundamentally simple. Complications come when we begin to involve the rational ego and try to explain energetic movements and truths using language that was never designed to explain such realities.

Quite simply then:

Everything within our reality has a time when it breathes IN, or absorbs energy in one way or another, and a time when it breathes OUT, or projects energy from itself in one way or another. Even things that seem to be completely static all the time, like perhaps a stone, have a time that they breathe IN and breathe OUT; it is just the case that with things like a stone such energetic movements are so slow (relative to our timeline as humans) that these things seem to be neither alive nor moving physically in any way. But all things are energy and therefore all things are alive in their own way, in their own vibrational frequency, which then dictates their own timeline of existence.

In order to manipulate energy properly, that is in order to shape the world in accordance with your Will, you must learn to use these IN and OUT fluctuations because it is through the understanding of them, and the correct use of them, that you can overcome any obstacle and defeat foes that are much larger and much more powerful than yourself.

Generally speaking, there will be a time when you project your Will and try to change something through Internal Manipulation, and there will be a time when you must absorb energy in order to defend against the attack of others, and gain more power from such attacks, so that you can increase your own Will Force (Potential); which you can then project in order to further increase the chance of getting what you want.

Since we are now, all of us, being attacked by this Alien Intent, we begin by absorbing this attack. We become Yin (which stands for the IN polarity), the passive polarity that is hollow and does not resist the onslaught that we all face. Beyond this, this polarity absorbs this attack and makes that energy that would bind us and feed off of us, our own.

You now know of the IN polarity technique as described in Chapter 4. We begin by fighting back against the Alien force by not fighting at all. Begin by actually absorbing the energy from the blow that has been hurled against us.

This means that we need to begin to absorb all the negativity all around us.

To do this, do the following:

Exercise: Negative Energy Absorption

The next time that you feel some kind of negativity, whether it is the negative feelings within you, or whether it is a negative emotion or aggression from those around you; absorb that negativity by pulling that energy into yourself instead of trying to block it or stop it some way.

> Whenever we come across any kind of negativity, whether it comes from ourselves or from the people around us, our first reaction is always to try to ignore it or to somehow block it so it does not affect us. Some people even try to use different types of psychic self-defence strategies, where they are taught to create some kind of shield around themselves or to flood themselves in white light or something

similar. All of these strategies rely on the basic premise that the way to defend against something is to block it in some way.

Psychic shields or force fields of one kind or another will not work in the long run. The creation of such shields requires energy and focus of attention which is very energetically draining. So unless you have an unending supply of energy, which none of us have, there will come a point when your shields will fail as your energy wanes. Also such shields cannot stop all attack; for example if such an attack is powerful enough it will go through the shield; think of it like trying to stop a car barreling at you at 100 miles per hour with a cooking pot lid.

Another favored technique to deal with the negativity of life is to ignore it. While it is possible to deal with some negativity by ignoring it so that you don't drain yourself and feed more energy into it through your attention, there is a point when you will have to face these problems because they seldom go away on their own; they only fester. Certainly, if this is some kind of mild negativity, there is the possibility that you can ignore it and hope that it reduces naturally in energetic power, and goes away in time. But quite often these negative things are powered either by a personal internal belief that cannot be ignored, or they are powered by external intent; like in the case when someone hates you, fears you, or wants to beat you at one thing or another. In such cases this negativity will only grow if it is ignored because it will have nothing to stop it from pooling into a massive energetic form.

It is far better to absorb the energy of any attack, or personal negativity that you might face. In this way that energy can be re-channeled into a far greater counterattack, or into changing the belief or life situation that is causing this negativity.

The best way to do this is to perform the same technique outlined in Chapter 4, but this time pulling not just psychic energy from all around you, but all negativity; sucking up all the negative thoughts, feelings, and intent that you and others are projecting.

You can even suck up negative situations so that instead of getting mad, sad, or scared when something bad happens, you suck up all the energy you can from yourself and that situation. You can tell yourself that you will pull IN all the negative energy that is causing this situation; and you do so using the technique I taught you in Chapter 4.

A good add-on technique that you can combine with the direct energy absorption technique is to use affirmations. For example, when you have a negative thought or are feeling negativity that you wish to absorb, you can say to yourself, "I take that energy into myself, I make it my energy and I drain this negative situation". With this affirmation your intent becomes quite clear and as a result it becomes far easier to absorb that energy that you wish to reclaim.

Two points that are most important here which must be considered very carefully when it comes to becoming an adept at this Alchemical absorption technique are:

1. In order to be to transmute this energy, in order to be able to take this negative energy and turn it into positive energy for yourself, **you need to be able to maintain a predatory stance.**

I speak of this predatory stance at great length in my book, *Vampire's Way to Psychic Self-Defense* but it is most prudent and necessary that I give you a synopsis of it here:

What I mean by the predatory stance is that you need to feel yourself becoming a bit of a predator when you are practicing this energy absorption technique. You don't need to become some kind of wild beast or a vampire of any sort, but you need to feel that the energy that you are absorbing is yours; that you have taken it from the world and that it is your food now.

This attitude is needed because in order to absorb all this negativity, especially the negativity of others and of the Alien Intent that powers most of this negativity, you need to beat and divert the current that drives this energy.

You see, energy is energy; there is no such thing as negative energy or positive energy. All is energy and all energy can be absorbed and used however you wish. Intent, while it is a type of energy itself, is like a tube that focuses that energy and gives it purpose; it is what turns it into good or bad from our human perspective.

In order to make use of this acquired energy, you need to first absorb that energy, but you also need to neutralize the power of the intent (focusing tube) that has shaped the flow and composition of that energy. You want to keep the energy and reshape the tube of intent that has been shaping it.

You do this by seeing yourself as a predator, as a ravenously hungry creature that takes what is offered by the world, and is now eating what it has caught fair and square. So as you absorb this negative energy, from wherever it might be coming from, feel it seep into you, and as it does so, own it, break it, make it yours, consume it for your own purpose, absorb it all and lick your lips when you are done!

2. **The absorption of ALL energy is prudent.** What this means is that even energy that is considered positive can often times be highly weakening. For example, some would have you believe that great outbursts of pure love or happiness will somehow allow you to get everything that you want, and that positive energy (who judges what is and is not positive?) can only create positive things.

The thing is though that this non-organic life that I speak of, that feeds on the distilled energy of humanity, is not just interested in negative energy; *it is interested in ALL energy*.

So you will see such non-organic predatory life feeding from war and tribulation, and you will also see it feeding in the midst of 'love ins', beautiful concerts, and anywhere were any kind of emotion is being expelled in great quantities.

This is so highly important and critical that I find that I must make it very plain and very clear. Great outbursts of positive emotions feed this Alien predatory life form as much as do outbursts of negative emotion.

Why then does this predatory Alien Force not fill the world with love and kindness so that it can feed and we can all be happy as well?

Quite simply, negativity creates strife that an organism must overcome and in the effort more strife is created, while love and joy create complacency which is really just another word for energetic inertia. If you want movement, if you want evolution of energy, you need strife. If you feed off of the energetic distillation of other aware life forms, the greater the strife, the better the energy distillation created; no strife equals sour food basically.

Also the reality is that negative emotions are far easier to create and they tend to be far more energetically satisfying because they are expelled from energetic bodies with a great deal of force, which is far different than the radiant energetic OUT bursts that are created from more positive emotions.

It must be understood though that losing yourself in some kind of loving outburst of emotional indulgence can be as draining to us as the outburst of negative emotion.

What you decide to experience and to absorb in your life is at the end of the day, your personal choice.

It is quite possible to ingest only negative emotion and to express all positive emotion as much as possible. In this way a person can have quite a happy life, absorbing all the negative energy around them and using that energy to create more positivity for themselves and others.

I'll let you choose what you WILL here, and only mention as a passing interest perhaps that Alchemists are interested in the absorption of all energetic flares. Alchemists are not interested in a happy life per se, they are far more interested in the overwhelming freedom that can be found by completely letting go of this vibrational frequency we call normal human reality, and the type of emotions that can be felt here. They are far more interested in the epic realms to be found Out There.

But what do you do once you absorb all of this energy?

Where does this energy go? How do you save it so that you can use it later as you Will?

As you absorb the blow of the Alien intent, what you need to do, as you feel this energy pulsating and moving into you, is to store it deep within yourself so that it can later be used by you effectively. Within all of us, at the very center of our body, there exists a natural collection point where we can store personal energy; it is here that you must store your energy.

The location of this collection point varies in people but it is usually around the same place where we imagine our stomach to be when we are hungry. This collection point can be used to store energy just like a type of 'Cauldron'. Indeed this is the ancient Alchemical cauldron which the 'Puffers' later believed was an actual real life stone and mortar or steel cauldron. But this cauldron is not an actual object Out There, it is a location within the energetic human bundle.

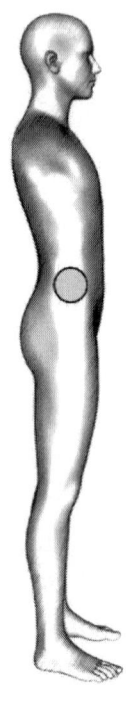

So as you suck the energy and negativity all around you, you should be able to feel a type of tension or perhaps even type of electrical vibration going through your body. Channel this tension into the very center of your body, into this Cauldron, and imagine that this tension pools itself there creating a powerful orb of shining energy.

You can help to anchor this orb of energy to this position by focusing your attention on it and imagining that it is becoming denser, more tightly packed, and brighter. With a bit of practice, you will be able to feel this internal Cauldron and the accumulation of your personal energy there.

By focusing your attention on this orb, you contain this energy and develop your internal Cauldron. This energy will then be packed tightly and will be ready for you to use whenever you need it. Don't worry if you feel that this energy has dispersed somewhat after you have not paid attention to your Cauldron for a while. This extra energy has dispersed through your body but it can easily be brought back to a powerful orb of energy through the act of focused of attention.

Keep absorbing more and more energy. Absorb all the negativity that you feel around you, in whatever way that you personally feel this negativity. Absorb all the negative thoughts that run through your mind, and all the negative feelings you might experience throughout your day. Absorb your doubt, absorb your ego (at least the negative aspects that you don't like), absorb all the negative things that you wish to get rid of, absorb all the negativity from others, absorb all the negativity from the world around you, and use that energy to fuel that orb that should be getting bigger and bigger within your Cauldron.

Maintain and purify this energy through your predatory stance by constantly telling yourself internally (and believing), that this is your energy that you have taken, that you have eaten, that it is nutritious, and that it is now ready for YOU to use.

Yours.

Your energy.

Now!

This is the Yin aspect of the Yin-Yang technique. We absorb the blow and take the energy from it into ourselves so that we may counterattack with it and win the battle.

Once we have a decent mastery over the Yin aspect, we need to move onto the Yang aspect by learning to extend our power. This means that we begin to exercise our Will Power, and over time our Intent, through the mastery of the OUT polarity.

CHAPTER 8, PART 1

Yang

**And make of them a marriage pure
Between the husband and the wife**
RIPLEY SCROLL

It can be very difficult to think about the idea that we are all food for an Alien force Out There. There is fear and perhaps anger which is understandable, but such emotions can be very debilitating. Such emotional indulgences can drain a person and exacerbate the real source of the problem, which is the feeling of utter powerlessness that such contemplations can create.

To feel powerless is the most terrible feeling that a person can feel, and the knowledge that this planet is in essence a type of prison planet, can drive some people mad. Perhaps it is for this reason that many secret groups, supposed enlightened groups, hide this knowledge from others. But I personally believe that this is a disservice to humanity and a great underestimation of human potential.

This is so because we humans are not weak or powerless, we have just never been taught how to be strong or why it is so important that we become stronger.

You see, Will or Will Force, which is perhaps the best known term for this OUT polarity, is an incredibly powerful '**counterpunch**' against the Alien Intent that now subjugates humanity. Through the mastery of the OUT polarity, which is the mastery of the personal Will, we are able to battle against the negativity that controls our waking mind, and through the correct conscious re-deployment of personal energy we are able to re-sculpt every aspect of our lives for the better.

If the IN Tri-polarity is our shield, then the OUT Tri-polarity is our sword, or our Magic Wand.

Will Power can be defined as the ability (the energetic strength required) to hold a particular view, and the ability to hold the focus of one's personal attention, on one particular goal, idea, thought, or desired event, long enough to be able to increase the intensity of energy present within

that particular goal, idea, thought, or desired event.

Will Power is the energy needed to maintain this focus of attention, so a better name for Will Power might be Will Force. In order to have strong Will, we need to have Will Force which we need to accumulate as raw energy from the world around us. This accumulation is something we have discussed in the last chapter when we learned about the Yin aspect of the Supreme Ultimate fighting art.

When we have enough of this raw energy (which is sometimes referred to as Potential energy) we can use that potential, that Will Force, to project energy. The act of energetic projection, using the mastery of the OUT polarity, changes things in two ways:

- it either changes one thing to another thing, which is the act of Transmutation

- or it creates a whole new thing, which is the act of Manifestation

The ability to transmute one thing into another thing is the basic ability that all Alchemists are looking for and it is the most recognized aspect of being an Alchemist. Famously, Alchemical transmutation is the act of turning lead into gold, but while such transmutations are possible for an Alchemist with enough energetic Potential, it is best to see these transmutations as a metaphorical ideal:

Changing lead to gold represents the ability to turn the gross into the sublime, the ability to turn a bad thing into a desired thing. As such, transmutation happens all the time, and the greater the Potential force of any one person has, that is the more energy that a person can accumulate and maintain within them, the more powerful that those transmutations can be.

In the most basic sense, the ability to change one thought into another is the act of transmutation. Imagine in your mind's eye a banana peel, and as you see it floating there in your mind perhaps, see it slowly turn into a lovely flower. I don't want you to superimpose a flower on top of the banana peel, I want you to slowly see that banana peel change shape and turn into a flower. If you are not a good visual visualizer you could imagine a sad feeling turning into a happy one or the feeling of a light rain on your head turn into a pleasant breeze on your face, The important thing here is to NOT superimpose one thought on top of another but to see this one thought transform from one thing to another.

If you try to place one thought on top of another, you are creating two thoughts and these will battle form dominance in your mind. If you transmute that one thought into something else then there is no battle and you are using the energy already present in the one thought to change it through your Will Power alone; this is transmutation.

Transmutation is energetically efficient. Masking is energetically inefficient and creates phantom thoughts that can plague the mind. So, the next time that you are trying to overcome a negative thought, you must try to transmute it, not mask it!

Manifestation is in reality Transmutation of a higher order. Often manifestation is used as a general term for any kind of change brought about through visualization or thought control of any kind. From an Alchemical perspective, Manifestation happens when a certain thought or idea goes from a really high vibratory state (like the vibratory state of a thought) to a much slower/denser one (like a physical object that you might run into). Manifestation is the ability to take a thought and make it real in accordance to human sensual perception; it the ability to take the thought of a flower for example, and turn it into a real objective flower that you and eventually other people can see, touch, smell, taste, and feel with their external senses.

The line between the Manifest and the non-manifest is actually pretty wide, and yet it is a very difficult chore to try and pinpoint exactly where that line is. When is something real? Is it real when you can experience it with your external senses? How many senses? Is it real when others can experience it through their senses? How many others?

If you want to see a flower and you are a very good visualizer, is that visualized flower real because you can experience it with multiple senses? Is it somewhat real because only you can see it?

If I ask you as a good visualizer to imagine a lemon, to imagine it being cut in half and squeezed so that the juices flow everywhere, is this lemon more real? Is it more real because you can now see this lemon and are now salivating as a result of this visualization?

Is something real when perhaps all people can experience it through their senses, not just you? But what if you are color blind to a certain color? How real is that color to you?

Does something become real when an authority figure says it is real? Are Moon landings and global warming real because scientists say they are real?

Or perhaps reality is created when many people can believe something? How many believers does it take to create reality?

A wide and tricky line indeed.

Manifestation is the transition from one side of that line to the other. A servitor for example, which is a thought that is given greater and greater form, that is greater and greater energetic mass, through finely focused attention, is perhaps the greatest example of a manifestation there is. Such 'Thought Forms' can perform relatively complex tasks, act in a frightfully independent way when they are not properly maintained, and can eventually even be seen by others when their energetic mass becomes dense enough.

In our everyday lives, it is possible to manifest just about anything depending on how much energy we have and how much energy we can project. The difference between a Manifestation and a Transmutation though is often most difficult to differentiate between and such differentiation is generally not worth the time spent on it; unless you happen to be deeply interested in the topic of mental power like I am.

For example, is that twenty dollar bill that you found a manifestation or a transmutation? Did that bill start out as a mental thought that became an actual physical thing because enough energetic mass was projected by you? Or was it placed in your path through a number of synchronicities that happened as a result of the transmutations of certain events? Is the twenty dollar bill that made its way into your pocket a thought made manifest or is it a bill that was always present but that flew your way as a result of synchronicity created by your Intent?

Whether transmutation or manifestations are involved, the OUT Tri-polarity concerns itself with all of this. This act of exercising one's Will is of great significance because with enough energy at our disposal, we can project that energy in order to create just about any internal (that is subjective) or external (physical) change we may want. The more energy we are able to propel into an idea, thought, event, or whatever it is we desire, the more likely that this one desired thing will come to pass.

When this desired event comes to pass, it means that a 'current' has been created Out There in the Dark Sea. A current created in the Dark Sea means that an internal desire has become an external reality; it means that the external Will of the Dark Sea has changed to suit the Will of the Alchemist.

Will therefore is the force that gives direction to our energy. It is the case that we can have all the energy in the world but if we do not learn to master our Will Power (which is essentially the OUT polarity), we are very much like a lovely shining star in the firmament; we shine brightly but we are stuck in an orbit that we did not choose.

And even the 'Illumination' that we might discover through the mastery of the VOID polarity is useless without the OUT polarity, because after we have discovered all this new knowledge, we must develop the ability to manipulate energy in order to turn this knowledge into true power and freedom.

As I have said, all polarities are important. We can't just have the ability to pull in energy and we can't just develop the ability to maintain energy and let go of the world, because that does not lead to a greater life, it leads to dissolution or energetic stasis. In order to truly evolve, we NEED a way to use energy to fulfill our full potential, because without this, illumination and self-awareness become a living nightmare; the nightmare of the beautiful bird stuck in a golden cage.

As supposedly self-aware beings that are in the process of refining our personal being, it is imperative that we take responsibility for our actions and our lives. By doing so we become aware of ourselves, our actions, and the decisions that drive us towards our greatest self-fulfillment. This journey towards self-fulfillment is really the journey towards learning how to manipulate energy through the focus of our attention!

Indeed, this journey is a natural one. It is a journey that asks us to become more ourselves and to work towards the realization of the greatest dreams. This journey takes us from the reactive non-self-aware creatures that most of us still are, to the fully conscious beings that we can become. In order to do so we need to stop acting like the world owes us something, we need to stop being so dammed unconscious, and we need to take full responsibility for creating the world that we want. We do this by taking responsibility of our energetic essence, and ultimately by taking responsibility for our internal actions; by taking full responsibility for the thoughts that run through our heads, and where it is that we place our attention.

There are many books written about finding out what you want. There are also many books written about discovering who you really are supposedly and how best to fulfill all your values, so I won't go deeply into this subject.

As far as doing the right thing, for an Alchemist all that truly matters is that he or she does the most energetically efficient thing. An Alchemist knows that in the grand scheme there is no good or bad, and yet from a human perspective, an energetically efficient Alchemist is always doing the right thing, even though he or she is never trying to be good, or bad for that matter.

This is so because impeccability (which is perfect Energetic Containment), is directly related to right/correct action.

Energetic efficiency/Containment = right/correct action

Also I think that it should be pointed out that, within all of us there is an almost unconscious understanding that there is more to life, and more to the fulfillment of our values, than endless happiness and the accumulation of material wealth. To fulfill oneself sometimes means that there is a part of us that wishes to struggle, and that there is a part of us that wishes to push itself to limits that it does not believe that it can overcome.

My personal belief is that you will grow a great deal if you use the power of the OUT polarity in order to develop skills that will allow you to have a better view of the human energetic condition, and of the greater Cosmos that surrounds us. Such practices can help us fulfill the spiritual desires. These skills can be developed by desiring and using the power of the OUT polarity to expand our awareness, so that we may become:

powerful thinkers, dreamers, and adepts at Out of Body Experiences.

Once we have a general idea of what it is that we desire, or at least a basic clue as to what we think might fulfill our lives, we have a direction in which to direct our **mastery of the OUT polarity.** We do this by **pushing OUT energy while focusing on that thing that we desire, and sustaining that focus of attention on the desired for as long as it takes to either transmute or fully manifest events or ideas. This is the Yang principle performed in an impeccable manner.**

In Chapter 6 I had you perform a number of visualization exercises to demonstrate the power of your attention. Such visualizations are the basic core of all energetic projection and they represent the practical application of:

thought + energy/chi/ki/prana/Vril/etc. = transmutation/manifestation

In describing how to perform these exercises you probably noticed that on a number of occasions I needed to use the word 'desire'. This, I hope, was a hint to just how natural all OUT energetic movement is. Quite simply then:

Desire is Action!

When we push energy OUT from ourselves, when we exercise our Will Power, we are exercising the most fundamental aspect of individual 'I' consciousness; we are desiring. As natural beings therefore we move energy through our desire:

Desire is Action!

When we wish to do something, no matter what the underlying emotion or lack of emotion is involved:

Desire is Action!

The act of desiring is the act of creating focus of attention. This internal action also quite naturally moves extra energy in the direction of the manifestation of the thing desired, and our emotions are also quite naturally rallied into this effort, making the act of desiring a very powerful act indeed.

By breathing OUT and by learning to focus the attention like a laser on one thing, while at the same time employing the feeling of desire, a person can bring a great deal of force to bear. This powerful burst of energy is the best way, in my opinion, to use the power of the OUT polarity to get what you want, whatever you want.

Using the three-part technique of:

- attention
- breathing OUT
- and the feeling of desire; in other words actively and strongly desiring what you want

will allow you to get whatever you want, dependent on how much energy you have been able to acquire and pump into that desired thing or event.

You desire in this way for as long as you need to desire in order to change the currents of that Dark Sea. Sometimes it takes a great deal of energy to change the currents of the Dark Sea, and sometimes such changes happen almost instantaneously. Knowing how hard it will be to change any one thing in accordance to your Will is an impossible thing to judge. The best that one can do is to do one's best, and to know that greater results will be achieved when one has impeccable mastery over the three polarities that allow one to pull in energy, contain it, and push it out with great focus and energy. All that is left then is the long road to personal evolution through value fulfillment.

There are many people who wonder why they are not able to get the results that they want when they practice certain mind power techniques. As I mentioned, most often the teachers that teach these techniques tend to only advocate the perfection of the visualization process, but they seldom mention the need to push energy into that desire and they seldom mention the power of desire itself.

And even when they do mention these things, they seldom mention the fact that all such successes in mind power techniques are due to the amount of energy that that one individual person has access to. I hope that I have been able to provide a far clearer explanation of what is involved.

Beyond this, I find it important to point out just what is happening when we project energy; that is when we use mental power, Will Force, to change something in ourselves or our environment. Quite often people assume that as long as they visualize long enough or with enough detail, anything that they visualize will come to pass. Such notions are flawed because they don't take into account the fact that most people have very little energy at their disposal. Most people tend to have far less energy than they suspect, as a result of a lifetime of energy consumption by the Alien Force.

Most of these modern classes on mental power, and even the more modern versions of magickal training, tend to completely gloss over any kind of energetic acquisition at all. Both modern manifestation techniques and schools of magickal practice do not teach people about the acquisition and the maintenance of energy. At most they tend to rely on the strengthening of their will through the evocation or invocation of some type of deity. While such techniques can work to some degree if they are done correctly, it is far better to learn how to acquire energy in a more direct fashion.

What is also seldom mentioned is the fact that all thoughts and therefore all acts of intention do in fact become manifest. Most though don't realize that not all Manifestations or Transmutations happen in what we would refer to as objective consensual reality. It is indeed the case that this one world is but one world of many, and our intentions within this world ripple across this world and across many others.

What this means is that just because something did not manifest here in this physically objective world in a way that we are aware of, it does not mean that it did not manifest in an alternate and more fluid reality. Oftentimes our intentions, that is the power of our Will Force, is not strong enough to bring about complete transmutation/manifestation in this world, but it can help to alter other worlds and indeed; our thoughts help to seed other universes that we are not aware of.

All our thoughts manifest to one degree or another whether we are aware of it or not. But if we wish to make sure that our intentions materialize within this world, this objective world where we all find a modicum of consensus, then we must strengthen our mastery of the OUT polarity.

In order to do this we must discover how desire becomes action and how we can use this power along with our focused attention and the control of our breath, to get what we want here and now!

CHAPTER 8, PART 2
Desire Without Compromise

Logic only gives man what he needs...
Magic gives him what he wants.
TOM ROBBINS

The act of life, the act of being alive, is the act of desiring. Sometimes this desire is not an emotional event at all and does not necessarily represent emotional dependence. Desire is a fundamental aspect of being a living creature; a self-aware entity within the Dark Sea.

A desire is representative of a deep internal need that every self-aware being is born with. Those desires have a direct relationship to continuing awareness and personal evolution, which is referred to as the desire for personal value fulfillment. This 'necessity' to fulfill personal needs and values is actually directly related to seemingly baser desires, such as the need for food and shelter. All desiring fulfills personal development and whether we consider such desires needs or values does not really matter in the end because all these desires move us forward.

Desire is the greatest evolutionary force in the world.

Desires though, are often seen as negative things. Perhaps one of the clearest examples of how much human desire is looked down upon can be seen in certain religious practices. For example, the Buddhist religion states that desire is the cause of all suffering, and one of its fundamental precepts is to get rid of all these desires in order to attain freedom through the dissolution of self.

But as I have said, to purge oneself of desires is to purge oneself of life, because the act of desiring is a natural consequence of being alive and self-aware. This is so because every single life form, as we understand the term, must push energy OUT from itself in the same way that human being must breathe OUT, which of course is the consequence of breathing IN. If this IN/OUT cycle stops, we die.

To stop desiring, to stop any one of the three polarities, means a truncation of energy that will destroy the living system over time.

At a base level, this 'desire' by some philosophies and religions, to stop desiring, comes from the 'desire' to stop losing energy to the Alien Intent. This technique of arresting desire is really a technique created to stop the Alien Intent from consuming our emotional energetic essence.

This Alien Intent puts thoughts in our heads; it creates seemingly foreign desires in our hearts. These desires do not create personal value fulfillment but instead are only designed to cause us more and more emotional stress, which this predatory Alien Life form then feeds upon.

The 'desire' to not desire is a reasonable thing when you look at it from that point of view. Such an admonition to stop desiring though altogether can't last forever and there will come a time when the desire to not desire will run out of energy. When this happens, all manner of mental aberrations will consume the person's mind.

In the best of cases, a religion teaches the practitioner how to meditate and how to use that extra energy acquired through non-desire (which is a form of Energetic Containment) to attain greater forms of personal ability and awareness through the use of the OUT polarity. Without these teachings, this type of religious practice becomes energetic stasis; which is a type of slow death. Unfortunately, such teachings within a religious context, are usually only taught to higher ranking members of special orders within those religions.

My personal belief, and one that I believe is shared by many Alchemists as well, is that discovering the difference between value fulfilling desires and those that are of Alien origin, is a most difficult thing and one that is for the most part a waste of energy. This is so because the intricacies of the Dark Sea are beyond the perceptive abilities of any human soul; whether that soul believes itself to be enlightened or not.

Within the Dark Sea we are but insignificant atoms within atoms, all a part of the infinitude Out There; we are nothing and the Dark Sea is everything. We cannot conceptualize how it is that we go about fulfilling ourselves or how it is that the Dark Sea provides for us those things that we might need to fulfill ourselves in the greatest way possible. The intricacies of the causality that it employs are beyond space and time and therefore beyond human judgment.

When you desire something, like some delicious sweet and decadent mouthful to quell your gluttony, or money meant to quell your greed, we believe these desires to be evil somehow. But these supposed evil desires might actually represent your best path towards personal value fulfillment and evolution. It is even the case that these seemingly 'bad' desires, and the ways that the Dark Sea satisfies them, or not, go about constructing a personal path and reality that not only fulfills us in the long run but also fulfills a part of the Dark Sea as well, no matter how little your individual intent is compared to the vast Dark Sea all around us.

As such, I ask you to take a desire, one that you have studied using your critical mind, one that you believe to be good for you and also good for all the people around you if possible, and I ask you to try and fulfill that desire with the best of intentions, because it is through the fulfillment of this desire that you will find the high road to Alchemical transmutation and personal freedom.

For example, let us try to refine the mastery of the OUT polarity by contemplating how to transmute into existence something that could be considered a long-term goal, such as having more money.

Since you have begun, I hope, by using the IN polarity, consuming as much negative energy as possible from the world around you, you now have removed this negativity from the world, which is a very positive thing in and of itself. Moreover, you may also have begun to store this energy so that you can now use it to better yourself and others. You have taken a bad thing in the world and now have extra energy that you can use to transmute/manifest something that you desire.

After you feel that you have a relatively large amount of this ingested energy at your disposal, what I want you to do is simply to follow your natural inclinations and just desire.

What this means is that, when we really want something, when we really need it, we begin to desire that thing. I therefore want you to take some time whenever you have time, in a quiet place preferably, and begin to desire that thing that you want.

How do you do this?

Well, think about for example of what it is like to desire delicious food.

Usually when we really want to eat something delicious we tend to focus a great deal of attention on it. If we have certain negative beliefs about the particular food that we want, we might berate ourselves for desiring this food, in which case we then desire not to desire. In all this manifold combination of desire, we release a great deal of emotion.

Desire happens all the time and it takes on many gradations of form, and as you might have guessed already; **the desire to cancel out a desire is still a desire**.

As a result of the many negative beliefs that we have about desires and the act of desiring itself, many of which are the result of the Alien Mind of course, we do not allow ourselves to naturally partake in this powerful but simple act, that would help us to get many of the things that would make our lives so much better.

Think about it, when was the last time that you let yourself just desire something without compromise? When was the last time you really let yourself desire something without feeling guilt of one kind or another?

Aside from these feelings of guilt, and the many memes about what is right and wrong, what often happens is that we always push ourselves into physical action as soon as possible.

We are all told from our infancy that nothing comes by wishing for it, that if you want something you need to work for it, and what this really means of course is that you can't get anything unless you work hard physically for it. This belief/meme is very prevalent because for the average person all that matters is external physical action. People are taught from a young age that the only thing that really works is physical work, and as a result few have ever tried to just desire those things that they want, and even fewer know how to desire properly.

I challenge you therefore to desire something, to wish for it with all your heart, without the need to take physical action in any way. Just engage in the act of desiring it with all you have.

This is internal action.

It is this internal action that is responsible for getting all the things we consciously want!

People can look back at their lives and rationalize how they got anything. Most often they will use a type of limited mechanistic causality to prove to themselves and others that it was only through physical work that they were able to get what they wanted. They will tell you that they weren't able to get what they wanted until they grew up, flushed away their childish dreams, and got down to hard work, in a manual and very 'no pain no gain' kind of way.

They often forget though, that in order to find a job, to find a creative way out of a dilemma, to invent something new, or even to find the will-power to be able to engage in all this physical labor for a long time, they had to desire all of this into existence, and they had to maintain that desire to be able to stick it.

They quite blindly gloss over all the internal drive, synchronicities (luck), and eureka moments that were the foundation of the manifestation of their desires.

The act of desiring is the force that allows us to consciously shape our lives, and these desires are a constant, whether we deny their existence or not. If you desire a job because you believe that this is the only way that you will get what you ultimately desire (money perhaps), then you will find that job in the manner that you desired to find it, and this job will be hard manual (or mental) labor if that is what you unconsciously desire. Because it must be realized that many of the bad things that come your way are the result of unconscious and sometimes not so unconscious desires.

These seemingly negative unconscious transmutations/manifestations created through desire, happen when we believe something beyond a shadow of doubt and cannot even contemplate that things could be different. Such a belief then is a blind belief; a belief that is hidden because even to contemplate that it might be wrong is unthinkable.

If you believe that hard work is the only way to big sums of money then you will desire that hard work whether you realize it fully at a conscious level or not. All of these desires will, to one degree or another, mold themselves into your personal existence in accordance with all of the forces that are affecting your life right now.

Personal Beliefs are the underlying structures that shape our lives, they control the direction of our thoughts and attention and if they are left unexamined, they will steer our lives in a certain unconscious direction. **Belief is the scaffolding of our lives, but desire is the enforcement arm; desire is the force, conscious or not, that turns dreams into reality.**

Some people will be cross because of my terminology here, they might argue that it is expectation not desire that gets you what you want. They might argue that it is the true expectation of a thing that makes it manifest, not the desire.

But this is a language problem again where it is hard to describe internal realities using a language designed for an external world:

From an energetic (that is Alchemical) perspective, expectation is a bridge feeling that begins to signal a change from personal Will to the Will of the Dark Sea.

It is the feeling that overcomes a person when their act of desiring is carried on long enough or is of such intensity that personal desire becomes a current within the Dark Sea.

When personal desire, which is Will Power, turns into a current in the Dark Sea, it means that desire (or Will) has turned into intent. A current in the dark sea represents a moving force that will push against and change the world. Desire has gone from being a personal daydream and it has turned into an actual force that changes the world, just like a wave might batter a coast line and change that coastline over time.

Intent therefore is desire turned into a law, a thing that must happen, an external force that will go out and change things in accordance with your Will. And **expectation is a subjective feeling that 'sometimes' indicates that this change from Will to Intent is happening.**

But it is very important to realize that Expectance is not an active force. A lot of people say, 'if you expect it, it will come, so expect it right now!' But Expectance is not a force, it is an intuitive feeling that you get 'sometimes' when you know when your desire has become intense enough energetically to transform itself into a command that the Dark Sea will carry out. So, when people say, "expect it and you will get it," what they really mean is: keep desiring even though you don't have any emotional energy to desire anymore because whatever you are doing, its working!

Expectation from that point of view is a variant of desire; it is the first hurdle that desire faces on its way to turning Will into Intent. Expectation here is what desire looks like when all the emotional energy behind desire is used up. Expectation is desire with little or no energy behind it; it is desire in the act of energetic build-up.

Expectation is a lukewarm version of desire; it is what desire looks like when all the emotional energy behind it is used up. Expectation expects, it knows beyond all doubt, and therefore has no need to push anything.

As many who practice any type of thought power technique know, everything that we do is a result of internal action:

from the people that we run into that either help us or hinder us, to the thoughts (creativity and intelligence) we have throughout our day, to the drive that we have, and most interestingly to that hard to pin down set of synchronistic situations that 'accidentally' happen, which we refer to as good or bad luck.

The part is seldom mentioned and understood is the fact that you don't create/make your complete reality; not totally anyway. Your particular world and your particular life are not just the result of 'your' Internal Action alone (your thoughts, Will, Intent, etc.). The world does continue to exist when you are not paying attention to it and it would have existed if you would have never been born. Moreover, the most powerful form of Internal Action, that shapes almost every aspect of human life, comes from a completely Alien Source.

This Alien Force that truly shapes the reality of life on this planet is actively engaged in directing the natural tendencies of human thought and therefore human Intent. It has reshaped the world in accordance to its own design so that it can construct a type of 'feeding trough' where it feeds on the energetic essence of humanity in the most ruthless fashion imaginable.

An Alchemist is first and foremost interested in overcoming this Alien Force and truly creating their own reality, their own perfect existence. He or she does this by refining his or her Will Force

through the most natural act of engaging in desire without any compromise!

To desire something into existence, to transmute/manifest something into existence using Will Power and Internal Manipulation, we need to do those things that most of the world will tell us are pointless, lazy, and non-constructive. What we need to do is to take the time to desire that one thing that we most want for as long as we can, without doing anything remotely physical to get it at all.

And then, only act physically when the perfect circumstance presents itself, in a way that makes it seem like this is what you knew would happen all along.

To act in this way is to get whatever we want without inciting conflict from others, no matter what the world believes to be possible. This is Internal Manipulation conducted in a perfect manner.

CHAPTER 8, PART 3

Dare to Desire

**But I've bought a big bat.
I'm all ready, you see.
Now my troubles are going
To have troubles with me!**
DR. SEUSS

In order to explain the power of 'Desire as Action' through the OUT polarity, let's contemplate the desire to lose weight. You have done a great deal of personal introspection, and as a result of what you believe to be your own personal values, you feel that you want to lose some weight. You might have a particular amount of weight that you would like to lose and a body shape that you would like to have, or you may not have any idea at all aside from the fact that you want to lose some weight; and the sooner the better.

So, take some time and desire losing weight!

Find a quiet place where you can be alone for a while, and desire the body and the weight loss that you would like to happen with all your heart. As you do so, you will notice that your attention will naturally focus on the thing that you want, and if there is emotional content associated with this desire, which there usually is, then this emotional energy will be naturally projected into that desire as well.

What this means is that through the natural act of desiring, you are focusing your attention, and you are also naturally projecting your energy into this thing that you want. This alone will go a very long way in getting you what you want through this process of Internal Action.

As you desire this weight loss, many thoughts will run through your head. You might experience different types of 'visual' visualizations where you might see yourself with the perfect body that you want at the beach perhaps, or you might see yourself surrounded by people admiring you and commenting on your healthy beautiful body. You might also experience other types of visualizations such as feelings of pride and the many other feelings that come along with having accomplished something that you set out to do.

Use the force of your desire to keep your attention fixed on these visualizations because the clearer that you can make them, the stronger that your Will Power becomes. Also, do remember that this is an energetic act, which means that it is an act of the OUT polarity. So, as you desire those things that you want, make sure that you breathe OUT in a long and steady OUT breath using, the techniques mentioned in Chapter 6.

Finally, try to desire this thing you want for as long as you can. If you will remember, I mentioned that Will Power required a sustained focus of attention. What this means is that you can't just desire something for a little while only to forget about it soon after. This desire must be sustained for as long as possible, and it should be the case that you should practice sitting around and desiring what you want on a regular basis; hopefully starting some kind of daily regimen.

You will find that this desiring business is not a difficult thing. There is something very liberating about being able to sit down and desire something without any guilt and without any compromise. So, sit and desire and open the floodgates of your feelings. After spending some time practicing Energetic Containment, this will feel quite invigorating.

If you experience negative emotions, rally those Energetic Flares into your desire, use these negative feelings to allow you to focus even more vividly on your desire; knowing the pain of not having should empower you to desire that one thing you want even more.

And when you feel joyous feelings as you naturally visualize in your mind's eye the materialization of your desires in physical form, use this emotional energy as well to flood those images with joy.

See if you can maintain this desire going for a good 15 minutes, then see if you can extend that. See if you can eventually spend a good half an hour or more desiring what you want.

As you try to desire that thing you want for an extended period, there will come a time when you will feel like you have just run out of juice. What this means is that the emotional need to lose weight will go away, it will feel like you will just be tired of all that desiring.

When this happens, what you need to do is to keep desiring without emotion. This is a very particular feeling that is hard to explain in words but that you can easily experience if you do dedicate yourself to desiring for extended periods of time. Desiring without emotion comes down to: telling yourself, in a dispassionate way, what you want, and then keeping the focus of your attention fixed on that desire. The focus of attention is crucial, just like it was when you were doing the visualization exercises in Chapter 6.

To desire without feelings is the first step to expectation. And when the final and true feeling of expectation manifests itself, it tells you that what you are desiring is becoming or has become a command...and then you keep desiring, in the most unrelenting manner possible until you get everything you want.

Desire in this unemotional fashion for a while, and try to maintain as much focus as possible. If you do this long enough, you will note that a flare of emotion might present itself again over time; that is, you might feel emotion again about the thing you desire.

When this emotion emerges, channel it into your desire as before until you perhaps find yourself emotionless again. In which case, you repeat the process as above, going from moments when your desire is backed by emotions and moments when it is not.

If one of these emotions becomes too hard for you to bear, remember that you have the power of the IN polarity at your disposal. If a certain negative emotion becomes too overwhelming and you can't channel (transmute) this energy into your desire, then make sure that you consume that energy using the IN polarity technique.

For example, as you are desiring weight loss, you lose focus and begin to think about all the delicious things you will miss out on or how hard doing all this is going to be so that you are momentarily flooded by great anxiety and a counter desire to do the opposite of what you wanted before. These emotions might become so powerful that you feel that you will burst into tears at any moment and you just don't have the strength to transmute these emotions into your original weight loss desire. What you need to do then is to consume these negative emotions; breathe IN and use the sucking IN technique discussed in Chapter 4 until you feel stronger.

After drawing IN this energy, you should feel a little more awake. This is an indication that a bit of extra energy is back in your body. Use this energy to focus once again on your desire. If these emotions return as powerfully as before, and you still feel you can't re-channel them, then suck this negativity IN again and then continue with your desiring. Do this for as long as your desiring session lasts.

This is the IN and OUT energetic cycle in action. It is the Yin-Yang of internal Mental Action.

Using this technique, you can accomplish anything. These techniques allow you to fight against the natural tendency of your mind to create an exact opposite of what you want. The mind, which is ruled by the Great Archon, needs the play of opposites to understand anything in its world: this is how reason works, without the play of opposites, reason cannot function.

This mental stance says: in order to know good, you must know bad. In order to know the true depth of black, you must know all of white. In order to know pleasure, you must understand the breadth of pain, and in order to know of weight loss you must know all the many ways that lead to weight gain.

This technique allows you to push through the barriers imposed by the mind. It does this by committing itself to the sustained focus of attention on the desire, and through the ability to re-absorb opposing energy which is then redirected into the desire as well.

In the previous chapter, we discussed some of the reasons why sometimes things do not manifest. We discussed the multiplicity of things that are involved in the transmutation of something from one vibratory frequency to another.

What we did not discuss so far is how much energy and attention are needed in order to manifest those things that we desire; we have not discussed the idea of increasing energetic intensity and mass.

There are two ways to achieve the intensity required to transmute (manifest) a thing, an event, or a silent command into existence:

1. Sustained Focus of Attention:

This means that you must keep your desire going for as long as it takes to get what you want. It is the act of silently and inconspicuously desiring without letting go of that desire. For a long-term desire, like losing weight, I recommend that you practice setting a time aside during your day to intensely and emotionally desire what you want on a regular basis. Beyond that, you need to desire that objective (like weight loss) continually, and use the techniques described earlier to re-channel all energy available into that desire in a sustained manner until you get what you want.

2. One Large Energy Burst of Focused Energy:

A ritual act, like a ceremonial magickal act for example, creates this kind of large energy burst. In my book, *Manifest Wealth and Prosperity with Thought Forms and Servitors*. I show you how to create this kind of concentrated energy burst without the pomp of ritual, and I discuss why this methodology is so powerful when it comes to dealing with the contrary forces found in the human mind.

This intensity increasing technique involves the combination of the focus of attention and the manipulation of natural energies within the Dark Sea. This buildup of energy comes to a crescendo as the practitioner takes this wave of intensely powerful energy and projects it straight into the desire; which might take the form of a mental visualization that represents the desire in in fully manifested physical form.

In this book, because of the fact that it is so deeply dedicated to the idea of overcoming Alien Intent and overcoming those entrapped by that Intent, we are most interested in increasing the energetic intensity of our desires using the 'Sustained Focus of Attention' technique.

Those who are trapped by the Alien Force have a meme agenda, are deeply interested in converting all others to their belief system and are deeply committed to enforcing those laws that their particular memes advocate.

It is impossible to confront all of these people openly because their large numbers. This means that they hold all the cards, and as anyone who has gone against the system will tell you, such an act is foolhardy and sometimes quite dangerous.

Internal Manipulation means internal action, it means performing an action that is not only more powerful and efficient than physical force, it is an action that is a completely secretive act as well. It is a type of action that you can do outdoors in public, in a way that no one will ever suspect what you are doing. It is a type of action that will allow you to work on the free evolution of your own life, of your own values/desires, without the fear that you will create any conflicts with all the people around you, who are, for the most part, living lives that are not their own, lives of emotional dis-balance; people trapped within the meme war.

Through Internal Manipulation you can create very favorable synchronicities (good luck) for yourself, you can accomplish all those goals that you always wanted to accomplish (no matter what others think of your goals or your chances of achieving them), and you can command others to some extent, depending on how much they have developed their own Will Power. This technique will allow you to begin to win all the battles that you may have previously lost!

You will be able to do this without having to hide behind some clandestine ritual chamber, and since this is a complete Alchemical system, you are also discovering how to access ALL of the power of the Energetic Sea that surrounds us, without the need for dark pacts with strange powers; that can be quite dangerous if done improperly.

In order to perform the techniques presented in this book having to do with the OUT polarity, it is imperative that you make a great distinction between External Manipulation and Internal Manipulation.

External manipulation is any type of physical action.

This means that any type of physical movement, *which includes body language of any kind*, needs to be kept in check if you want to perform Internal Manipulation in the presence of others. Instead of letting your energy escape in physical movement, you need to focus on a type of action that takes place completely on a subjective level, without ever revealing the fact, in a physical way, that anything extraordinary is going on at all.

In order to explain this better, let us consider how we might use the OUT polarity to try and attain a more short-term goal, one more in keeping with the many conflicts that make up our day to day life.

For example, we might consider using the power of our Will Force to get a store clerk to treat us better, or perhaps use this power to get a good seat at a coffee shop or restaurant.

Let's say that you are returning something at a department store and you happen to find yourself face to face with an employee that has been rude to you in the past and who always makes trouble for people returning things, even though store policy clearly states that it is within your right to return said item.

First of all, generally speaking, a face to face confrontation with such a person will almost always just make things worse. If you confront a person like this:

a person who is possibly very much lost within the dark clouds of Alien Intent, someone who is negative and is in a constant war with others, determined to spread some kind of meme or another as much as they can...

...you will only lose your energy.

The world is full of people like this, people who are constantly negative (or over the top positive), who have totally given themselves over to upholding some righteous agenda. This kind of person is quite literally looking for something to push against.

If you confront a person like this then you give them the fight that they need so desperately, and the only thing that you will be doing when you push back is losing personal energy and giving this person an even greater reason to treat you badly and try to rip you off.

This does not mean that you have to look at every interaction that you have with other people as a type of battle. It is quite possible that you will run into many people throughout your day who will have a good outlook and a pleasant demeanor, but there is always the chance that you will run into those who are particularly interested in pushing their meme no matter what.

When you do run into those kinds of people, I would suggest to you that you use the Alchemical techniques that we have discussed thus far, specifically the techniques of Internal Manipulation and the Yin and Yang of mental action.

You do this by not giving this person something to push against, by giving them no place to attack. You become hollow or empty and pull IN, in that place (or in that way) where they would be

inclined to attack you, and you become solid and you push OUT your energy by focusing your efforts on Internal Manipulation instead of External physical action. In this way, you counter their attack in a manner that they can't defend: you perform an Internal Attack.

Through this Supreme Ultimate technique, you can topple very powerful opponents by pushing against them with a counterattack they won't suspect. You can think of this counter as a type of 'Soft Push'.

So, when you confront this particularly difficult clerk, do not engage in any kind of physical response to their negative and impolite aggressions. Instead, focus the greater part of your personal energy into the act of Internal Manipulation.

This means that you should resist verbal debates, wrinkled brows or any other kind of aggressive physical action or body language that will only cause this person to become even more territorial. Instead, what you need to do is concentrate the greater part of your energy on absorbing their unpleasant energy using the IN technique and countering with a Soft Push by strongly 'desiring' the outcome that you want; first absorb, then project.

You can look at this person, just don't stare. And as you look at this person with a calm and perhaps completely unemotional face, strongly desire that this person will treat you with respect and that they do indeed refund the item that you are returning without any conflict at all. There is a careful give and take here: you don't want to feel too much emotion or else you are going to explode. I personally would recommend that you absorb as much of their negative energy as possible and that you then try to project your desire in the most emotionally controlled way possible for you.

Also, don't get stuck trying to absorb and project energy at the same time. If you try to do both at the same time you will cross your wires as it were, and you might lose your composure. Just remember: absorb, project, absorb, project.

Finally, don't interest yourself in revenge or beating the other person down. Concentrate your efforts on getting what you ultimately want, which in this case would be a pleasant experience in which you are easily able to return an item that was not to your liking for one reason or another.

In these circumstances you are, if this is indeed a situation that has become negative and confrontational, quite literally pitting your Will against the Will of Others and the Will of the Moment.

But instead of fighting a pitched battle through physical action and direct confrontation, a battle where the only winners are those Dark Forces that are interested in consuming both yours and the clerk's energy, you rob this dark intent of its power, you consume the negativity of others, and you impose your own Intent if the situation deems it necessary.

These kinds of internal battles are always going on. We are all having conversations, debates, and very heated arguments with one another on a telepathic level. Often, we are, for the most part, completely unaware of these internal conversations that we all engage in because we lack sensitivity or because we just can't bring ourselves to believe that such things are possible.

By taking conscious control of your own energy, and by consciously directing your desires upon the world, you can become very adept at winning these silent battles which often mean the difference between a pleasant life experience, and a life of constant anxiety and intimidation.

Yes, as you might suspect, the projection of energy through your desire does mean that you are giving the Alien Force some of your energy. It is important therefore to choose your battles carefully and exercise your Will only when you think it is necessary. If you have to give up your energy, then do it for something that you feel is worth it. Strive for freedom and the perfection of your life, instead of trying to beat others and impose your memes in an effort to save the world or dominate it.

The world is perfect as it is; it is an impeccably created place where we are given the chance to transmute base material into the purest gold. A place where we learn how to perfect our ability to manipulate energy.

This after all, is the true Magnum Opus of human existence.

CHAPTER 9
VOID the Final Frontier

The key to growth is the introduction of higher dimensions of consciousness into our awareness.
LAO TZU

This book went through a great deal of evolution in my mind as I contemplated and worked on my vision of it. It started out as a way to fight against the system, as a way to finally begin winning instead of being in a constant state of frustration and pain.

It became obvious quite quickly though, that such a book was dis-balanced, which as an Alchemical practitioner myself, would not do.

The dis-balance was due to the fact that I meant to only present one particular polarity, the OUT Tri-polarity, and ignore the other two. Such a dis-balance is acceptable at times and my books generally tend to favor one polarity above the others. But that would not have worked with this book because it would have become quite dark and aggressive. This would have made the book a lopsided view of human reality, which is of no help to anyone in the long run.

The world is already full of a great deal of aggression; wherever you look there is always someone pushing against someone else, or one group battling against another for dominance. This dominance is almost always a meme war where one set of beliefs is fighting against another.

If I had just presented the OUT polarity in the way that I would have wished to, I would have been perpetuating this meme war, and the only player that ultimately wins that war is the predatory Alien Force that now controls man's fate.

Using just the OUT polarity, there is no winning a meme war because even if you try very hard to live a good peaceful life, focusing on only having good thoughts about yourself and others, trying very hard to not push your beliefs on others, you are still expelling energy that is feeding a megalithic predatory non-organic life form Out There. This Archonic force will use every trick in the book to get you to expel more and more energy over time. As such, you will find it very difficult to realize your dreams because:

1. You are not full of infinite energy. Sooner or later your powers will wane as you expel more and more energy but have no way to replenish what you have lost. Even if you save energy by not pushing against others and just concentrate on your own life, your attention and focus of mind will diminish over time. Few of us have the focus of attention needed to try and be happy all the time, but even those who have such skill will eventually run out of energy if all they know how to do is push energy OUT.

Thinking a certain thing and not thinking something else requires an expenditure of energy. Paying attention to one thing and ignoring something else requires energy. Once our energy wanes, as it must, we lose that focus and fall from whatever height that we might have attained.

2. The intent of others counts; you are not alone in this world. Contrary to what some might believe, you cannot ignore the world and expect it to leave you alone so that you can have all you want without any cost at all. Something must always be given or pushed against in order to get something else, nothing is free.

Even if you ignore the tiger, the tiger will not ignore you, and his desire to find food is as strong (usually stronger actually) as your desire to find peace. You cannot ignore those things in the world that you don't like or don't want expecting that they will somehow go away and leave you alone.

3. There is an external predatory force Out There. It advances its agenda, which is to consume human energy, by imposing a dis-balanced perceptive view on all humanity. This perceptive view is designed to make every human being on Earth expend as much emotional energy as possible. Whether those emotions are fear, hate, worry OR love, compassion, joy, ecstasy. To this megalithic being, it ultimately doesn't matter what emotion it is as long as it gets plenty of it.

If you are constantly indulging in either loving or hating, you are ultimately losing.

Because of these obstacles, I have acquainted you with both the IN and OUT polarities together in this book. With them you can consume the negative intent (push) of others, even that most powerful Alien Intent of the Archon, and turn that into personal energy which you can then transmute into personal change. In this way, you move through the world as a powerful force; this time winning the many battles that we must all face while on this Earth; through the principles of the Yin-Yang of Internal Action.

But those are just two polarities within a Tri-polarity system, and while there is a bit more stability now, and certainly a winning strategy for beating all the foes on this Earth, there comes a point when you begin to question why you are fighting so much in the first place.

Perhaps through hard work and focused effort, you might be able to get most or all of the things that you want. You might be able to feel that you are winning, there might be even a 'lofty' few who might be able to say, "I have it all...but now what?"

The answer to this question is revealed when we strive to master all three polarities in equal measure.

And it is through the third polarity, the VOID polarity, that we find an escape from the final challenge of our existence. It is only through the mastery of this final polarity that we find out where and how the battle is truly won.

The mastery of the VOID polarity is, quite literally, the doorway to another world. It is the doorway to a greater reality and greater truths. But this doorway cannot, and should not, be opened completely until we have mastery of the other two polarities first.

The first aspect of the VOID Tri-polarity is its ability to provide peace and contentment, the ability to detach us from this world of seemingly endless conflict. **Through the use of the Energetic Containment technique, we are able to discover a type of relaxed happiness that is not otherwise possible in this chaotic world.**

Our world is in a constant state of flux as energies are being propelled one way and another through what would be termed natural phenomenon, or natural forces. The striving of all humanity and even the striving of that Alien Force that feeds on us, are all NATURAL phenomena in that we are all the children of the Dark Sea.

This constant flux is outside of us and within us as well. Outside, we see great movements of the Earth and its inhabitants, we see stars shift and change, we experience the seasons and the weather, and people move and evolve. Inside, we feel emotions, needs, desires; we experience thoughts, feelings, and transcendence as we grow old and evolve through the medium of time.

This flux is life can be very invigorating, but it can also be very tiring and very hard. Sometimes the constant flux of our lives seems to bring us nothing but pain and we can often conclude that most of life is nothing but suffering.

Energetic Containment allows us to stop all or a great deal of this internal fluctuation of energy; it gives us a way to stop some of the suffering. It is the energetic technique by which we can transcend a particular stage in our life, and grow beyond our previous limits.

While it is the case that we may not be able to control the colossal forces that are beyond any human Intent, we are nevertheless able to control how these titanic forces affect us to some degree.

Energetic Containment gives us peace and an odd joy. This joy seems somehow like a contradiction in terms though, because instead of trying to PUSH ourselves into feeling happy all the time, which gets tiring very fast, we become happy and joyful by not trying to be happy or joyful in any way at all. We discover joy through Internal Silence.

Because Energetic Containment is so powerful and important, let us consider the act of walking through a large crowd of people; which some can find very difficult.

This is because there is a psychic weight to people, that can be really hard for some to take. The more people that there are in any one place, the heavier this weight becomes. In large crowds everyone is PUSHING this way or that, all trying to do their thing while at the same time following some kind of mob/group energy that unites them all, that can propel that mob/group into unified action with devastating force.

The next time that you find yourself in a large crowd, perhaps in a large really crowded mall, see if you can maintain Energetic Containment in this place.

Exercise: Energy Containment While In a Large Crowd (Energetic Containment Level 1)

- Start by just relaxing your body as much you can. This is always the best way to start because as you might have noticed, we often tense up a bit every time we find ourselves close to people, especially large crowds of people. So, as you are making your way through a crowded mall, you may find that you become somewhat tense.

This tension is quite natural because the body will instinctively prepare itself for the unexpected while in the presence of so many people. One could say that for the body to not prepare itself for the unexpected while in large crowds, would be the unnatural thing to do.

- It is therefore a good idea to begin by taking a deep breath, filling your lungs completely, and letting go of this full breath in the most natural sigh possible, making no effort at all to hold that breath in. Once you are in the midst of this large crowd, start by taking three deep breaths like this and making sure to let those breaths go, by relaxing your body completely and letting your body expel that air naturally, as a nice relaxing sigh.

- Now consciously try to feel your body and try to notice if there are any areas where your body is still tense. If for example, your shoulders are tense, I want you to consciously focus your mind in that area, bring your conscious attention to those tense shoulders, and tell yourself internally, "Relax".

Do this with any parts in your body that seem overtly tense. You can do this in matter of seconds once you get the hang of it.

- Next, I want you to use that pulling in force I mention in Chapter 4, when I had you try to pull in a cup placed on top of the table. Use that powerful pulling in force to pull IN the energy that you feel you are projecting from yourself. Note that if a part of you was quite tense then this means that this part of you has accumulated energy like a kink in a hose and is most likely now projecting energy OUT into the environment. I want you therefore to use that pulling force to try and pull that energy back into yourself. Pull with as much force as is required to pull all that energy back into your body.

Start by pulling in from those tense spots in your body, and then from those areas that you feel are projecting energy more than others. Eventually see if you can pull in from every single part of your body so that you feel like you are pulling in from every pore of your skin. This kind of conscious control of the energy that you are expelling takes a bit of work, but once you get the feel for it you will be surprised how easy and natural it all becomes.

Feel that force coming into yourself; concentrate on pulling IN your expelled energy. Try to forget about the people around you and just focus on your own energy.

- Once you feel you have created a type of psychic wall or separation between your body and the rest of the world, I want you to become aware of this wall. I want you to focus your attention on this psychic wall, on that barrier between your self-contained energy and the energy that is flowing all around you.

When your attentions is focused on this wall, I want you to try and solidify this wall with your Will. Focus your attention on it and imagine that it is becoming more and more solid, that this barrier is becoming harder and harder.

- Now try to walk through the crowd while maintaining this Energetic Containment field. If you feel that you have expelled energy beyond your Containment Field, perhaps because some person gets in your way and you get mad or something catches your attention and makes you react emotionally in some way, I want you to use that pulling force to pull that energy back into yourself again. Once that expelled energy is back within you and it feels Contained again, remember to solidify that wall and continue with your walk.

Do this for as long as you can, and see if you can walk through the entire crowd in this fashion.

What you should be able to notice quite quickly is that a walk that might usually leave you drained and frustrated will not be so debilitating at all. This absence of an energy drain is what most people notice right away, and it can be quite startling to note just how much energy you usually waste when walking through a large crowd of people. The usual reaction that I hear from people that have tried this exercise is that they are amazed to note just how much life energy is given up through human interaction.

Besides the invigorating feeling that comes from Energetic Containment, the second thing that some people notice can be far more startling.

As a result of the separation that they have established between themselves and the world around them, some people can begin to strongly feel the energetic waves of the Dark Sea for themselves. Energetic Containment will allow you to begin to really feel the energetic tides as they crash against you. This feeling is very much like being lightly pushed by wave after wave of this tingly energy or tension that seems to push against you ever so slightly.

And as people feel this displacement of energy around them, they can start to truly feel that we are indeed surrounded by an endless sea of energy. Some people can become so good, so quickly at detecting this energy that they are even able to feel the waves of energy that are generated in these large groups of people; they can sense this flowing energy as it leaves these groups and crashes into them!

The final and perhaps the most rewarding thing that you will notice as you separate yourself from others energetically, is the great clarity of mind and the calmness of your emotions. Through this calm separation from the flux of life, a deep internal joy begins to overcome you, which grows in intensity the longer that you are able to maintain this separation through Energetic Containment.

Joy and happiness then become your natural state, as long as you are able to maintain your Will focused on the act of Energetic Containment.

I personally use Energetic Containment any time that I need to act impeccably. Thanks to Energetic

Containment, I am able to think and act clearly in situations where I need my logical mind and the ability to act precisely without hindrance from my emotions.

I would not be overstating things when I say that this technique has changed my life. It is my deepest wish that it can help you as well.

It is said, even though I personally have not experienced this myself, that if you can 'Will' Energetic Containment long enough, that your Will eventually becomes Intent. This means that this separation between yourself and the world around you becomes permanent; it becomes the Will of the Dark Sea. At that point, you are no longer part of the human race; you have become a being apart and are free to ascend beyond the struggles of the average man.

While this is an amazingly powerful consequence of VOID polarity manipulation, there are more gifts to be gained through the use of this polarity. In this first part we have used the first aspect of the VOID polarity, which is directly related to the prefrontal cortex of the brain, and have thus attained mastery over our impulses and emotions. This ability when it is completely mastered negates a great deal of the influence of the predatory Alien Force and allows the practitioner to stand alone in the flux of human chaos.

In the second VOID polarity technique, we engage an even more powerful procedure that directly influences the Pineal Gland or Third Eye as it is referred to in many mystic philosophies.

VERY IMPORTANT:

The Pineal Gland is a 'Stargate' that opens doors to other places and dimensions, and Melatonin is the fuel that makes it go!

In this second exercise, I want you to engage the VOID polarity in order to not only stop your energetic flares, but to completely stop all the mental chatter in your mind!

In order to do this, you need to take advantage of a natural mental propellant available to all of us, if we are willing to go through the trouble of cultivating it. This particular hormone is called melatonin and it is the hormone responsible for making you feel sleepy. This is the hormone that takes you from the waking state into the dream state. This hormone is produced by the Pineal Gland which is the physical aspect of the Third Eye that is often spoken of in mystic literature, and this is the location of the VOID polarity in the physical body.

Exercise: Silencing the Mind through Melatonin Build-up (Energetic Containment Level 2)

In order to cultivate this hormone and use it to stop all internal dialogue, I want you to use the second technique that I showed you in Chapter 5. Now that you have a greater understanding of all the polarities, let me refine this technique slightly:

- I want you to simply make sure that you take at least fifteen minutes out of your sleeping cycle every day. What I mean by this is that if you sleep for a total of eight hours on average every night, I want you to reduce that sleeping time to seven hours and forty-five minutes.

- My personal suggestion to you is that you remove this fifteen minute period of sleep time from your morning instead of your evening. I recommend this because the use of melatonin in this way can reduce the amount of this hormone that is present in your system. If you use up this stored melatonin in the evening, you might not be able to sleep after; which means that if you take fifteen minutes off to do this exercise before sleep every night, you will most likely have a hard time getting to sleep afterwards and might go through bouts of insomnia.

- So, if for example you use an alarm clock to wake up every morning at seven o'clock in the morning, I want you to put your alarm clock back to six forty-five. In this way, you are giving yourself a full fifteen minutes of extra time in which to do the technique that I will describe shortly, and at the same time you will be increasing the melatonin in your system in a gradual way. This extra melatonin can then be used to increase the power of the following technique and to help you relax throughout the day.

> Remember this special note:
>
> Please to not try this kind of exercise if you drive or are in charge of any kind of sensitive/heavy equipment. Lack of sleep can greatly reduce motor skills and reaction times, so please do be careful and only perform these exercises if you feel that you can safely engage in them.

- What I want you to do is to use these fifteen minutes and the extra melatonin that you have at your disposal to completely shut off your mental chatter. You do this by using those extra fifteen minutes to mediate in a most unusual way.

- When your alarm rings in the morning, I personally suggest that you sit up in bed and make sure that you feel somewhat awake, and set your alarm back to seven so that you don't sleep in.

- Ideally it would be best if you could sit up in bed so that you do this meditation in a sitting position. If this is not possible, I want you to lie back down on your bed and bring your knees up so that if you do begin to fall asleep again, your knees will fall to the side and this movement will hopefully wake you up.

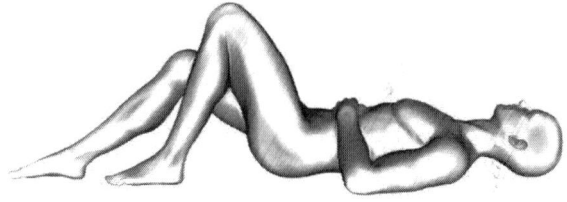

- What you are doing basically is that you are engaging in a type of hypnopompic exercise [see glossary for definition].

- At this stage, there is a tendency to want to fall right back asleep and to instantly start dreaming again. I want you to fight against this tendency for now. That is why I recommend that you sit up in bed for a complete minute when you awaken at six forty-five, and please remember to use this minute to reset your alarm clock so that you don't sleep in. This should wake you up just enough to allow you to perform this technique correctly. After you feel more awake, you can lie back down if this feels more comfortable but remember to bring your knees up as I recommended.

- Instead of giving yourself over to sleep and dreamland, I want you to try and focus on the feelings that you might be experiencing within your body. In particular, I want you to focus on that drowsy feeling that seems to indicate a great need to fall asleep. This drowsy feeling is caused by melatonin and it is this feeling/hormone output that I want you to exploit. Pay attention to this drowsy feeling and concentrate all your attention on it.

- You will note that as you concentrate your attention on this feeling, your internal chatter will completely stop. If you pay real close attention to this feeling of drowsiness as it moves through your body, you may also begin to feel this drowsiness like a tingling sensation. This numbing sensation will move up and down your body and will have a tendency to become most noticeable in your head. This feeling will eventually feel like your head is being anesthetized, like it's going numb. And this is exactly what is happening; it is a numbness of the brain, a numbness of the cerebral cortex. This numbness, will allow this part of your brain to slow down so that you are able to engage deeper parts of your psyche.

Indeed, **melatonin is the doorway to other dimensions**. It is the doorway to what we refer to as dreams. These 'dreams' are really jaunts by the human consciousness into different dimensions, outside of physical reality.

- But at first, I do recommend that you stay away from these dream jaunts for a little while and instead focus on the feeling of complete quietude of the mind. In this exercise, I want you to focus on that numbing feeling and use it to your benefit in order to stop your internal mental dialogue.

- It is quite likely that you will fall asleep because it becomes very difficult to maintain focus while in such a drowsy state. Hopefully when you fall asleep your knees will fall to the side and this will prompt you to wake up again. When this happens, I want you to once again try to focus on that feeling of sleepy drowsiness and continue like this until your fifteen minutes is up and you must get up for real.

- In a relatively short period of time, you will be able to maintain that drowsy feeling for long periods without falling asleep completely. By doing this you will be engaged in complete internal silence for extended periods of time, which will allow you to begin to explore internal dimensions beyond imagining.

- Eventually, you will be able to remember this feeling of silence and replicate it while you are fully awake during the day. Do be careful though as this can be a dangerous exercise if you need your wits about you, as you may become drowsy during the day.

This ability to silence your mind completely will quite literally create a vacuum within you, and this vacuum will separate you from the objective three-dimensional world some call true reality. In time, you will be able to maintain this complete silence while at the same time have a different part of you stay conscious and awake in the 'real' world. While one part of you engages in this objective three-dimensional world, another part will partake in odd adventures within fluid dimensions inside strange angled rooms that have no walls.

This type of general mastery over the VOID polarity is what allows you to enter into your dreams. It is the manipulation of this polarity that I use when I engage in my internal explorations and my Out of Body travels, as I have related in my earlier book, *Out of Body Experiences Quickly and Naturally*.

Mastery of this polarity not only creates internal silence, it opens the door to other realms that you can begin to explore if you so desire.

Together, the three polarities working in a balanced way, allow a human being to develop his or her full potential. While the IN and OUT polarities allow a person to be able to powerfully manipulate within whatever dimension they might find themselves, the VOID polarity is the one that allows a person to open a dimensional door beyond this one dimension that most people are trapped in, and enter other just as valid dimensions of existence.

Together they are the Holy Trinity of Alchemy, and their mastery is the only possible way to attain the Magnum Opus!

Conclusion

I hope that I have given you a good introduction to the Holy Alchemical Trinity. I have done my best to try and present each one of these polarities and the techniques that go along with them as succinctly and as immaculately possible.

The knowledge of The Holy Trinity, and the active desire to master these three polarities, makes you an apprentice in the TRUE art of Alchemy.

And a general capacity with The Trinity makes you an Alchemist proper, especially if you have acquired enough energy to begin to re-shape your reality, slow down your aging, and are beginning to move beyond this three-dimensional existence.

It is my hope that this book can start you on, or help you continue on, this path to true freedom.

I would personally recommend that you spend most of your time engaging the IN polarity, especially if your regular day involves a great deal of interaction with others; so about 70 to 90 percent of your day.

Use VOID polarity 'First Level Energetic Containment' when you need to act critically and precisely, or 'Second Level Energetic Containment' when you feel you have enough energy to move beyond this three-dimensional cage; perhaps 5 to 10 percent of your day.

And use the OUT polarity when you need to face memetic zombies or when you need to re-shape your objective reality; so perhaps 3 to5 percent of your day.

These suggestions are subjective of course, if you spend a great deal of time with people or if you spend most of your time alone in creative projects, then you can change how and when to engage any one polarity to your best advantage.

Whatever time frame you choose for any one of the three polarities, do remember that the OUT polarity is the most energetically costly so do use this polarity wisely. Remember, energy acquisition and conservation is the number one enterprise of all TRUE Alchemists!

The techniques covered in this book are of course not even a scratch upon the surface of all that these polarities can be and are, within the science of Alchemy. There are incredible subtleties within the energetic movements available, and using them to their full potential would take lifetimes of effort.

The IN polarity for example can be refined and its power used to extend physical life for a long time. The OUT polarity can also be refined and used to remake and manipulate any aspect of reality, so that a master of this polarity could quite literally create whole new worlds in which to inhabit. And as you might have guessed, refinement of the VOID polarity allows one to escape the confines of this physical world and move through space, time, and the boundless dimensions available for an eternity, if the traveller so chooses.

I feel though that this one book provides all the knowledge needed to begin a true Alchemical journey for anyone who can turn this knowledge into power through their Will/Intent.

If you have read any of my other books then you will note that any particular book deals with the mastery of one particular polarity:

- Create a Servitor: Harness the Power of Thought Forms = OUT Polarity

- Create a Servitor Companion = OUT Polarity

- Manifest Wealth and Prosperity with Thought Forms and Servitors = OUT polarity

- Vampire's Way to Psychic Self-Defense = IN Polarity

- Out of Body Experiences, Quickly And Naturally = VOID Polarity

Each of these represent ways to refine an aspect of the Tri-polarity.

This book then becomes a type of binding agent that brings all those books together by presenting the underlying forces that are discussed in each one of them.

This book is not an ending certainly, but it does represent a beginning towards what the old Chinese schools of Alchemy refer to as "Lian" or "TiLian", which means refining of the ingredients.

This book is a greater refinement of 'The Work' thus far presented; the beginning of a movement towards greater understanding of the powers available to those who wish to evolve beyond their current limits/cage.

This book IS a true Alchemical treatise, and this book in combination with the five books

mentioned above represent a complete Alchemical Grimoire.

This book is the foundation for a complete Alchemical system, one written in plain language without riddles or codes.

To speak so plainly of things that were held in such secrecy in the past is liberating and represents the continuation of the energetic confluence of these modern times. This energetic confluence dictates that all things that were once hidden shall be uncovered, so that the only thing standing in the way of any person's evolution is the power of their own individual Will.

This means that in these modern times knowledge can no longer be hoarded for wealth and power, and this is a good thing. But it does mean that greater responsibility is put on the individual, and that individual's ability to use the knowledge available; that individual's ability to truly turn knowledge into power.

It is my hope therefore that you test and refine your Will Power. Use the power of your focused attention, to refine the OUT polarity as presented in this book through the power of 'Desire as Action'. Furthermore, once you begin to see positive change in your life, I hope that you use whatever extra time and energy you have to refine the other two polarities as well.

Fulfill your life as your inner desires beg you to, and in this way naturally refine your own spirit essence. And do realize that as you fulfill your personal values within this world that we all share, and help to create, that you are also helping the whole of mankind to fulfill itself as well.

Every person that fulfills his or her personal values and eventually overcomes the predatory intent that has hitherto limited them, widens the path of freedom for all those who follow. By widening this path you make it easier for others to follow in your footsteps, and every act of illumination helps the whole of humanity to grow.

This continues until a tipping point is reached, a critical point where the number of people going through some kind of Alchemical transmutation is so great that it literally forces the rest of humanity into a more evolved state, which propels all of humanity into the next step in our collective human journey.

So to bring this treatise to a final end,
And briefly to conclude all these secrets here,
Diligently look at, and attend to your figure,
Which contains in it all these secrets
great and small,
And if you conceive it, both
theoretically and practically,
By figures and colours, by scripture plain,
It wisely conceived, you may not work in vain.
SIR GEORGE RIPLEY'S RECAPITULATION OF THE TWELVE GATES

Glossary

belief structure — A type of complex subjective scaffolding that is made up of the beliefs that any particular individual might have. This gestalt of beliefs supports and seeds the manifold compartments that make up the human mind. As such they are also the structures that determine what will be perceived, what will be ignored, and how all this perception (or lack thereof) will happen.

causality — The relationship between cause and effect. Contrary to what many believe, Alchemists contend that there are many different types of causality models and that each causality model opens up a whole new world of possible perception and action.

cognitive position — The point that defines how an aware being structures thoughts, experience and sensual data. There are an infinite number of cognitive positions, and each one provides a different world view that can be somewhat different or completely different from another.

Dark Sea — The Darkness Out There, that surrounds this world and all possible worlds. It is an energetic sea made up of mostly darkness, with splashes of light and aware life thrown in to the mix. We are all born of the Dark Sea and we all return to the Dark Sea.

energetic/emotional flare — A large burst of energy, usually caused by a strong surge of emotion.

Great Archon — A titanic predatory non-inorganic life-form that descended upon the Earth millennia ago. This megalithic shadow being from the depths of the Dark Sea feeds on the distilled energetic essence of humanity, and certain other 'higher' order life forms that also exist on this planet. The Archon does this by projecting an incredibly powerful telepathic signal that invades the awareness of every single human being on the planet.

This telepathic signal superimposes a foreign mind in the consciousness of human beings and funnels human awareness into a very limited range. Even though this foreign mind gives humanity the gift of self-awareness, it also takes from humanity by controlling the thought content that humanity experiences. This thought content guarantees that humanity is full of doubt, fear, anger, hatred or any other emotion that generates the most energetic flares possible; including many emotions that people consider highly positive like, blind love, pity, compassion, and righteousness.

The Great Archon cannot be beaten through physical force, it can only be beaten through the mastery of the Holy Trinity.

Holy Trinity — A TRIAD of energy polarities found within the human energetic structure. Through this Triad, humanity can interact and become part of the Dark Sea that surrounds all of us. This Trinity is perhaps the most misunderstood aspect of human existence and has given rise to all sorts of dogma, metaphor, and ritual. Alchemists dedicate their lives to mastering the Triad, as this is the only way to rip the gift of individual awareness away from the Archon and fly away towards true freedom Out There in the outer cosmos.

hypnopompic — Generally defined as a state that immediately precedes, or leads toward, the waking state. In this book, it means the act of maintaining the focus of attention (and therefore awareness) on this threshold state in order to open a door into other dimensions of existence.

Illuminatus — This quite simply means 'one who has become illuminated'. Within the context of this book, it means that this person has become aware of and believes or is beginning to believe that the world is indeed more predatory and far stranger than they had ever suspected. Beyond this, an

Illuminatus is someone who, as a result of these changes in cognitive awareness, is no longer truly a part of the everyday world that most human beings experience.

Impeccability — The set of actions, both internal and external, that allow for the greatest conservation of personal energy. From a bystander's perspective, impeccability looks like goodness, refinement, politeness, good will, and good old-fashioned values. But from an Alchemist's perspective, impeccability means detachment, control, discipline, analytical thinking, forbearance, prudence; which represents the totality of a life lived as an expert in Energetic Containment.

Intent — A current of energy created outside of the human energetic structure, that is able to change aspects of the Dark Sea. The Dark Sea changing itself through the behest of a powerful Will(s).

Internal Manipulation — The ability to manipulate energy, and therefore reality, through actions that are completely of a subjective nature. Manipulation through action that is non-physical.

meme — a belief that is passed from host to host in a similar way to a contagion. "An idea, belief or belief system, or pattern of behavior that spreads throughout a culture either vertically by cultural inheritance (as by parents to children) or horizontally by cultural acquisition (as by peers, information media, and entertainment media)" [urbandictionary.com]

Memetics — "Memetics deals with information transfer, specifically cultural information in society. The basic idea is to conflate the exchange of information between people with genetic material, to track the mutation of ideas as they are transmitted from one person to the next in the way you could track viral transmissions and mutations. However, a meme also provides benefits to the carrier if they spread it." [scp-wiki.net]

Schrödinger's cat — Erwin Schrödinger was a Nobel Prize winning physicist who contributed greatly to the then emerging field of Quantum Physics. He is most famous for a thought experiment coined "Schrödinger's cat":

A cat is locked in a sealed box with a small amount of a radioactive substance. Inside the box there is also a radioactive detector that is set to release a poisonous gas if it detects any radiation decay. After one hour there is an equal probability of one atom from the radioactive substance either decaying or not decaying. If the atom decays, a device smashes a vial of poisonous gas, killing the cat. However, until the box is opened and the atom's wave function collapses, the atom's wave function is in a superposition of two states: decay and non-decay. Thus, the cat is in a superposition of two states: alive and dead.

[www.britannica.com/biography/Erwin-Schrodinger]

So, in this one point in time, to an outside observer, the cat is both alive and dead at the same time. The only way for the observer to find out if the cat is either alive or dead is to open the sealed box, and collapse the wave function through observation. This wave function collapse by an outside observer is in my opinion a good illustration of how Quantum Transistors works.

Technological Singularity — Generally refers to the invention of Artificial Intelligence and the unstoppable technological growth that this will bring about. Within the context of this book, the greatest threat that this Technological Singularity poses has to do with how these new technologies will begin to affect and quite literally dominate native human consciousness.

Perhaps the greatest threat comes from the introduction of human cerebral implants that will begin to collectivize all human thought. This collectivization of human thought will most likely end Free Will, as we currently understand that term. At this point, I theorize that escape from the Great Archon will be impossible.

Transmutation — The ability to change a subjective experience into objective truth or the ability to do the opposite. The ability to move energy from one vibratory state to another.

will force/power — Energy (of varying amount depending on how much a person is able to store) propelled within the human energetic structure through the focus of attention.

I hope you enjoyed this book.

If you would like to receive occasional emails when I release new books and interesting information, you can join my private mailing list.

johnkreiter.com/mailing-list-sign-up

For questions and comments, you can reach me though my site at
johnkreiter.com/the-three-great-secrets-of-alchemy

Or though Facebook at
facebook.com/johnkreiterdotcom

Thank you for reading.

Printed in Great Britain
by Amazon